A Sicilian Martyr in Nagasaki

Calogero Messina

A Sicilian Martyr in Nagasaki

Translated into English by Helen and Peter Dawson

LEGAS

© Copyright Legas 2002

No part of this book may be translated or reproduced in any form, by print, photoprint, microfilm, microfiche, or any other means, without the written permission from the copyright holder.

Messina, Calogero, 1945-
(Jordanus non est conversus retrorsum. English)
A Sicilian Martyr in Nagasaki. / Calogero Messina ; translated into English by Helen and Peter Dawson.
   p.cm.
ISBN 1-881901-32-7
1. Giordano, da Santo Stefano, Saint, 1598-1634. 2. Christian saints--Italy--Biography. 3. Christian saints--Japan--Biography. I Title.
BX4700.G68 M4713 2002
282'.092--dc21

2002005785

Original title:
Jordanus non est conversus retrorsum, Edizioni Internazionali di Letteratura e Scienze, Roma 1998.

On the cover: *The Trial of Brother Giordano in Nagasaki,* detail of a painting by André Ribes.

For information and for orders, write to **Legas** at the following addresses:

P.O. Box 040328	3 Wood Aster Bay	2908 Dufferin Ave
Brooklyn, New York	Ottawa, Ontario	Toronto, Ontario
11204, USA	K2R 1D3 Canada	M6B 3S8 Canada

To my parents
Unblemished witnesses
Of long gone simplicity
And of faith
Strengthened by sacrifice.

Table of Contents

Prologue ································· 9

I. What Did the Children of Santo Stefano Do? ············ 11

II. The Miracles Worked by Brother Vincenzo of Santo Stefano ···· 17

III. The Convent Was a Second Home for Him ················ 23

IV. Even the Spaniards Came to Love Him ················ 33

V. *Jordanus Non Est Conversus Retrorsum* ················ 39

VI. The Missionary Center in Manila ···················· 49

VII. The Miraculous Image of Our Lady of the Rosary ············ 53

VIII. Who Could Take His Place in the Philippines? ············ 57

IX. Japan, Land of Martyrs ···························· 69

X. He Looked a Real Chinaman ························· 75

XI. Like a Dove that Knows not Where to Come to Land ········· 79

XII. How Could He Bow to One Who Had no Respect for God? ···· 87

XIII. She Too Had the Right to Die with Her Father Giordano ······ 91

XIV. Whom Are You Ordering to Trample on This Sacred Image? ·· 95

XV. *Dux Aliorum Martyrum* ·························· 99

XVI. Return ···································· 101

To Saint Giordano of Santo Stefano ···················· 105

Prologue

The majestic crest that climbs on high, straight and solemn, rolling gently up to the peak of San Calò, has always evoked in me thoughts of eternity. At the top stands a little church which the devotees of the old Hermit visit every year, to keep watch over him. They embrace him as if he were one of their own, and they fall asleep at his feet.

The mountain peak looks down on the smiling valley of Magazzolo. The foothills stop just beneath it, seemingly fresh cut, glistening white, high above the dark green below. The ridge plunges more quickly down towards the countryside, sloping away to the valley. The first houses in Santo Stefano Quisquina cling tight to the soil, the yellow bell-tower of San Nicola, like a wild asparagus plant, rising loftily above them; the chiming of the great clock gently marks the inexorable passing of time in the town and the surrounding countryside.

How many tales these places could tell! The stones speak of the simple, homespun Saracens. The mountains and valleys appealed to the Norman hunters, and they were also admired by Rosalia Sinibaldi, the Hermit Saint of Quisquina.

In the days of Emperor Charles V, a wondrous child ran happily over those pastures. Of the honored Traina family, he decided to become a Dominican friar, and later, now Brother Vincenzo of Santo Stefano, he departed from his hometown and Sicily to go far away to Bohemia, where he preached the Roman Catholic religion. But he returned and after his death was revered as a blessed soul and invoked for his miracles, until he was forgotten.

Those were centuries of hard existence, of endless pain, of hatred and death. The barons were arrogant, brother against brother, each intent on annihilating the other: *Blood Valley*, near the town, recalls their deeds. Those who were in their power had to put up with it and say nothing. And more tragedy came when it was decided to unite Italy so that all might have a better life. Those were days of revenge; men were stoned to death, as Saint Stefano was, and there was a massacre even at Christmas. But life did not change, even after Italy was united.

Most of the people in Santo Stefano continued to live in abject poverty: orphans left to themselves who did not know why they had been born; old women abandoned by everybody, even by their own families after these had taken all their possessions; men who had toiled all their lives but could work no longer nor do anything for their hungry children; and women agonizing in their shame. And they died with no hope of any better destiny for their children or their children's children. No one had a word to say of them.

Don Lorenzo Panepinto, a Santo Stefano man of generous heart, decided to open the eyes of these underprivileged people, to give them a voice and free them from their masters' torment, to tear them away from the claws of the rent collectors and the moneylenders. He said he wanted equality and brotherhood, like Jesus Christ. He was murdered outside his house, one May evening, as he waited for the moon. More blood was shed by his avengers, and by his avengers' avengers. Now they all rest below the peak of San Calò.

How many shattered hopes! The second millennium was drawing to a close and no one in Santo Stefano spoke of the greatest of all the town's sons, everyone's hope, another Dominican friar born the same year that Father Vincenzo died, who also set out on a long journey, an even longer one, from which he was never to return.

I.
What Did the Children of Santo Stefano Do?

Life went on in the same old way for the men of that land, a land protected by a crown of mountains rich in water, pastures, and vegetation. High up among the mountain peaks, the farmers and shepherds carried on the tasks of everyday life, as their fathers had done before them and as their own children and their children's children would. They were accustomed to a life of sacrifice and could never have imagined anything different. They were themselves part of the countryside, along with the animals and the plants.

And they would listen to the murmur of the waters, the rustling of the trees, the singing of the birds, the tinkling of the cow bells, and the tolling of the church bells, as they spread their sweet melody: the wind carried these sounds far afield. The town too was immersed in the countryside, and the men never left their animals. Even inside their houses they would listen to the braying of the donkeys and the whinnying of the horses and their stamping, the crowing of the roosters, and the bleating of the sheep, and they were used to the constant chirping of the crickets, the whistling of the wind, and the howling of the wolves.

The Spaniards were still there, as in the rest of Sicily, but no one felt their presence. The people of Santo Stefano, the Stefanesi, continued to go about their daily tasks, and many of them seemed more like Saracens than Christians, even if they lived by the laws and rules of the Holy Roman Church, in the most rigorous conformity to the norms laid down by the Holy Council of Trent.

The archpriest, Don John Pérez and Cuellar, was a Spaniard too, but what was he supposed to do in Santo Stefano when he could not understand a word of what the local people said? The Stefanesi wanted their priest to be one of them: it was not just a whim, it was a necessity. And soon they were granted what they had long hoped for. Don John's term as priest did not last long and he was soon replaced by a man from Santo Stefano, Don Vincenzo Minardo. Not that there was a lack of priests in the town! There were the Dominicans and the Carmelites too.

In the churches the inhabitants of Santo Stefano found moments of consolation and hope, and relief from their hard work and daily misery. Everything was for the family, all the toil, the quarrels over property, the grudges that lasted a lifetime and were passed on from father to son.

In a house in that hamlet lived Master Vincenzo Ansalone with his family. His forebears had been no less than lords of Santo Stefano, and he had had, and indeed still had, many powerful relatives in half of Sicily. However, for him, the best times were long gone, as happens sooner or later in this world; his father, Don Sipiuni — may he rest in peace! — had died many years ago, before he married Lavinia. He was a Master, and that was still a respectable status; there were but few masters in Santo Stefano, as elsewhere, for it was not an easy title to obtain: so many longed for it, workers and apprentices! But it was as if an *adduvatu* had aspirations to become a *massaru* or *curatulu*.[1]

An apprentice not only received nothing from his Master — he even had to thank him for taking him on. The Master's workshop was more than a school; there an apprentice received a good education and learned how to live, how to behave with other people, how to grow to be a man, so that after a few years he could look forward to becoming a workman. After a trial period, a workman could apply for the qualification of Master but it was no use if he did not have someone behind him and a bit of money — and of course he also needed to be very good at his trade. The workman had to pass a test in which he showed what he was able to do: you could not talk your way through it. He had to present a piece of work he had done. If he passed the test and obtained the qualification of Master, he could open a workshop and register it in his own name. However, it was not sufficient to be able to work as a Master and have the qualification. You still needed money — there was a tax for taking the exam and there

---

[1] *Adduvatu*: a boy or young man who worked for a landowner; *massaru, curatulu*: men entrusted with the running of a farm.

was a tax for opening a workshop. A Master's son, on the other hand, could open a workshop and work as a Master without taking any test and often without even having to pay the normal tax. You also had the same advantages if you married the daughter of a Master, as the Master's qualification was part of the dowry. But who could afford to marry a Master's daughter? A farmer or a shepherd could not dream of it. And so the son of a Master would become a Master himself; and the son of a farmer or a shepherd would always be a farmer or a shepherd.

Lavinia, Master Vincenzo's wife, also belonged to a family of Masters, the Di Salvos. They had given her an unusual name for Santo Stefano. Her father, Master Nino, had also died: she was already an orphan when Master Vincenzo had taken her as wife. He was around 23 years old, and it was the last day of February 1588. The following year Donna Maria, Master Vincenzo's mother, also died. Lavinia had not been lucky with her children either: Francesco and Gianfrancesco both died a few days after they were born, but then she had had Sipiuni and later Giacinto.

On the first day of November 1598, in the Church in Santo Stefano, the Reverend Don Vincenzo Di Marco baptized some children, among whom was Master Vincenzo and Lavinia's last child. They had named him Giacinto, in honor of the Saint of Krakow, who had been canonized four years earlier. The Dominican Fathers had made the Saint popular everywhere, even in that village lost in the mountains — and many people in Santo Stefano had given his name to their children.

Giacinto's godparents were Judge Gianfrancesco Bertolo and his wife Palma Di Trapani. That same day one of the judge's children had also been baptized. The judge was well respected; he had plenty of property — houses in the Maddalena area of town and a piece of land that gave him all he needed. The Di Trapanis were also a family of Masters and were on excellent terms with Master Vincenzo, as was only right, as Masters were supposed to get along well with each other. And there had already been some precedents that linked them: in the same year that she was married, Lavinia had stood godmother to Angela, the daughter of Master Vincenzo Di Trapani, the catapan. And Palma, or *Parmuzza*, as she was known in Santo Stefano, loved being a godmother — but only to those who deserved it, that is.

To be in mourning was not a rare occurrence in Master Vincenzo's family. When Giacinto was not even two years old, he lost his mother, in September 1600. She was buried in the Dominican church. Master Vincenzo wept for her, but he was not a man to let things get him down and even on this occasion he took courage and married again. His new wife was a woman named Margarita, some fifteen years younger than he. But it was only right that women should be much younger than their husbands, it had always been so.

The children in Santo Stefano were little Giacinto's first little friends. What did the children of Santo Stefano do? From a very young age, they were all curious and impatient to get to know the places where they were born and where they were going to have to live. As soon as they were able to go off on their own, they would rove around the countryside; *round the seven farms and the seven mills*, their parents would say, half worried and half pleased.

They climbed the mountains to learn their secrets. The peak of San Calò was always a good reference point and they would draw it on the wet ground with an awl or a nail, or on the walls with a piece of coal or chalk. Or they would use a thorn to draw it on the flat branches of the prickly pears, the plant the Spaniards had brought from a faraway place, Mexico. They would watch the sun at sunset, and the moon as it rose in the sky, large and beautiful over the peak, looking like a man's head with eyes, a nose, and a mouth.

They never wanted to stay at home: the houses were too small for them. They loved to go and play in the countryside, where they could be free. They also went down to the rippling river. They gathered up clay, slapped it on stones, and then molded it with their little hands. They would almost invariably make it into goats or cows or donkeys, the animals they were used to seeing.

They pulled branches off the trees, cut the twigs, and made little bows to shoot at the birds. They shook the palm-trees to bring down the dates, and they took the broadest parts of the branches, which were the tenderest, and turned them into boats that they would send off down the turbulent river. They carved pieces of wood in a thousand ways and turned them into awls, crosses, and daggers. They cut bamboo canes to make little flutes. And what about the elegant giant fennel? This they turned into stoppers, lattices, bird cages and many other useful things for the home. In various ways they cut the branches off the prickly pears and fed them to the goats.

Most of them were been born to be *adduvati* or farm hands and help their elders. They did not even need to be told: they immediately wanted to do what the older children did and would spend all their time in their company. With them or even on their own, chasing away from their mothers, they would go looking for asparagus or snails, and then take everything back home. Even their games had to serve some useful purpose. They even organized their own celebrations on Saints' feast days, with processions, bands, and fireworks.

Giacinto missed his mother: nearly all his little friends had a mother. When the mountains roared with thunder and menacing darkness crept down into the valley, or when they heard wolves howling, they would run back home — Giacinto could only look for comfort from his father. But death came also for Master Vincenzo, again in the month of September, when Giacinto was not yet sixteen. He too was buried in the Dominican church.

II.
The Miracles Worked by
Brother Vincenzo of Santo Stefano

In Santo Stefano, in Palermo, and indeed all over Sicily, people spoke of the miracles worked by Brother Vincenzo of Santo Stefano. He had died on 4 May 1598 and Giacinto was often told about him.

Brother Vincenzo was born in 1525. When he was seven, his parents granted him his dearest wish: to go into retreat in the local convent of San Domenico in order to become a Dominican friar. When he was fifteen he was duly admitted into the Order and he took his vows in the convent of Santa Zita in Palermo. He was also commissioned as a lector.

His life was one long act of penance: in his food, in his drink, in everything really. He bound his sides in a hoop of steel, which he wore throughout his life: he only took it off a few days before he died, throwing it into a well, so that nobody would know of his penance. He was constantly reciting his prayers to himself.

He was a Visitor, a Prior, and a Master of novices. He also traveled far afield from Sicily, all the way to Germany, where he was affiliated to convents of Bolzano and the province of Bohemia, which at the time was torn by religious strife. He spent his life trying to persuade people to follow the decrees of the Holy Council of Trent for the triumph of the Holy Roman Church.

He had been respected and admired everywhere, and left great memories of himself. He did so much for the convents in Termini, Catania, Caccamo, and Polizzi that they had to build another dormitory to satisfy the demand of boys who wanted to become Dominicans. He returned to Sicily for good in 1594 and once again he was Master of novices at Santa Zita and Subprior, until his death.

Brother Vincenzo suffered greatly from his ailments, and especially from an ulcerous boil, but he never neglected his duties. He brought comfort, the word of God, and life wherever he went, and people would ask for him with the greatest of faith.

A woman called Maria was about to give birth, and she was lying very ill in bed. The doctors could do nothing. A nun from Santa Zita suggested they should call for Brother Vincenzo of Santo Stefano. The friar went to see the sick woman; he sat by her bedside and spoke sweet words. He blessed her and encouraged her: if she had faith she would be saved. He then took his leave and made toward the door; Donna Melchiorra Cangelosi, who had been caring for the poor woman, ran after him and asked him what he really thought of her condition. And Brother Vincenzo repeated to her that she must have faith, for Maria would be blessed and she would have a baby boy whom she was to call Vincenzo. And so it was, as many were to tell, that Maria had a fine little boy and called him Vincenzo.

Donna Melchiorra never tired of repeating how, a month before Brother Vincenzo died, she had developed a swelling in her throat which remained until the friar died. She had then gone to Santa Zita and rubbed on her throat some of the lime mortar that sealed up the friar's tomb: two days later the swelling disappeared.

It was especially after he died that many came to understood what Brother Vincenzo of Santo Stefano had been, and they proclaimed the favors they had received through his intercession. His body was displayed in the middle of the church of Santa Zita and his devotees came from near and far in a never-ending procession, to pay their respects, to touch him and kiss him, and to ask him for favors.

On the very day of Brother Vincenzo's death, Paolo de Silvestro's wife, who was suffering from a terrible pain in the stomach — she could not rest and felt as if her whole body were afire — went to Santa Zita and obtained a piece of his habit. She placed it over her stomach and immediately the pain vanished.

Sister Caterina, of the Third Order of St Dominic, had a violent pain in her shoulders, and could not turn or move one way or the other — she suffered agony night and day. When she heard that Brother Vincenzo had passed away, she immediately asked to be taken to him at Santa Zita; she knelt down and kissed his hand again and again and prayed earnestly for grace. She then listened to the sermon, and the words of the preacher — a true thaumaturge! — increased her devotion, but her pain grew stronger than ever, and with it came a great heat that made her sweat. She started to cry, but after a while she felt she was healed. When the sermon was over, she made her way forward through the crowd to thank Brother Vincenzo and cried out she had been saved by a miracle.

Another nun of the Third Order of St Dominic, Sister Margherita, had had a swelling in her body for years and years; the doctors called it a "disease of the flesh", but could not cure her. The poor woman also suffered atrocious pains in the head — she said she felt like a windmill — as well as asthma in the chest, and she had no rest night or day. On the morning of Brother Vincenzo's death, she went to Santa Zita and stood in front of the body laid out in the middle of the church; with great devotion she took the hem of the habit of the holy Father and wrapped it round her body, begging to be delivered from her pain. She felt a great commotion in her body, and had to go straight home, where she evacuated almost half a barrel of water. She ran all the way back to the church of Santa Zita to shout the miracle.

Another nun walked up through the crowd. She had a heart condition and a great pain that never left her and tormented her to tears, and she could not bear the voice of other people. She kissed the hand of the dead Father and prayed with great faith: in an instant she felt she was healed.

The news of those extraordinary happenings began to spread, and from all quarters of the city, from Monreale, Santo Stefano, Girgenti, and from every part of Sicily streams of people, many of them sick, made their way to Santa Zita, where the Friar was buried, to ask for favors and to get a piece of his habit or of the bandages he used to wrap his sores or to scrape some lime mortar from his tomb. And many returned home crying that their requests had been granted and that Brother Vincenzo was a Saint. In the end, at the Diocesan Curia in Palermo they began to interrogate the people who had been miraculously healed and the process for beatification was initiated. Nobody had any doubt of its outcome. But all those who had known him and received favors or just heard of him could not wait to venerate him, and his image already began to appear in several different places with the qualification of Blessed.

A man was seen striding along quite normally who before could neither walk nor stand without crutches and who could only crawl on his stomach when he put them down. People stopped him and asked how it was possible, and he declared that Brother Vincenzo had healed him, a few days after his death, when he had lain down on his coffin.

Donna Antonia Rao was the wife of the most illustrious President of Justice. At home she had a black servant, called Valenziana, who had hurt her groin as she was doing the housework. A lump as big as a lemon had appeared. Valenziana could not move her leg, the right one, and was in great pain, and as she could do nothing she stayed in bed. Her masters had put her through various treatments, but the doctors could not find a remedy and eventually they had been clear: she would never get better. Donna Antonia had preserved with great veneration a bit of lime from Brother Vincenzo's tomb. She had a pageboy take it to Valenziana, so that she could devoutly drink it in a cup with some water. The servant drank it and immediately fell asleep. When she awoke, both the lump and the pain had gone.

Donna Antonia also declared that she had a small fistula in an eye. She had shown it to the doctors and they had treated it many times, but to no avail, and the problem was getting worse. She took some of the lime and put it on her eye. The eye started to discharge matter and little by little got better, by the grace of Brother Vincenzo.

Notary Mariano Rizzo suffered from a violent headache and his throat, the right part of his jaw and his right ear were full of dreadful sores. He had also gone deaf. The doctors' cures did no good and the sores were spreading. When he heard that Brother Vincenzo from Santo Stefano had died and that he had performed many miracles, he made his way painfully to Santa Zita. He heard Holy Mass with great devotion and then went to the place where the holy Father was buried. He took his handkerchief and rubbed it on the tomb and then on his face and throat, where his ailment was. After a few days his headache stopped and the sores dried out. He kept the handkerchief as a relic.

While in the Church of San Domenico, the surgeon Don Bernardino Scarso Ursino had developed a pain in the left side. A pimple had started growing there which now was as large as an ostrich egg, and even bigger. He had made some medicaments of his own but they had not worked; nor had the suggestions of other doctors. He remembered that Brother Vincenzo from Santo Stefano had died. So he called for Father Leonardo and asked him for a piece of the holy Father's tunic. Father Leonardo asked another friar to bring it to him, and as soon as Don Bernardino laid it over the pimple, he saw it shrink away and he felt no more pain.

Donna Virginia had had sores on her body for a year and they caused her a great deal of pain. The doctors had given her a number of things to try on them, and in particular the residue of crushed olives, but they been unable to find a remedy. So she went to Santa Zita with her mother. She entered the chapel where Brother Vincenzo was buried and licked the coffin with her tongue. She also took some of the lime from the wall above and took it home. She ground it up into powder, put it in a cup with some water, and drank it: this remedy immediately caused the sores to disappear.

Donna Agata Garbata was also ill in bed and could not sleep nor sit up in her bed nor get up. When she had to leave her bed, the pain almost made her pass out and she was forced back into bed; she trembled and threw up any food she was given. A number of doctors — Matteo Corvino, Pompeo Ferraro and others — had given her various cures but to no avail and Dr Corvino had said she would certainly die. Even the doctors suspected that the trouble might be caused by a spell. Brother Vincenzo had just died and the woman was brought to Santa Zita in a chair. They put her next to Brother Vincenzo's sepulcher and she knelt down and prayed that she might either recover or die. She stood up and walked home on her own two legs and saw that her illness had abandoned her.

People lost count of Brother Vincenzo's miracles, which were verified and recognized by the most illustrious doctors and surgeons. The members of his confraternity often invoked him, even in their moments of temptation, when they were tormented by the devil. They would hold his sackcloth in their hand — some would even keep it at their bedside — and the devil would leave.

Brother Vincenzo had many relatives in Santo Stefano and all his fellow townsmen talked about him and looked forward to seeing him as a Saint on the altar.

III.
The Convent Was a Second Home for Him

The Dominican Convent of Santo Stefano stood at the foot of Monte San Calò. It was called the Convent of the Most Holy Rosary and was located two kilometers from the village. It had none of the comforts that the Dominicans enjoyed in their other convents: indeed, they had once abandoned it because it lacked so many of the things that are necessary for a normal existence. But after a while, in 1602, they had returned to it and adapted it to their needs: now seven friars could live there, with a certain dignity. There was renewed enthusiasm in the convent, an enthusiasm that spread from the convent to the whole village and the country all around.

Giacinto had started going to the convent when still child. He was attracted by it and he was the friars' heart and joy — there he found warmth and hope, for the convent was a second home, as he no longer had his mother, or his father for that matter. The friars told him of his relatives who had become Dominicans — of Father Francesco Ansalone of the Convent of San Domenico in Palermo, who was the son of a man of considerable influence, the famous Paolo Ansalone, a Senator of Messina, defender of the motherland against the Turks; of Father Vincenzo Ansalone — named after his father he was!; of Father Domenico Ansalone; and of Antonia Ansalone of Messina. And they told him of Brother Vincenzo Barresi of Polizzi, who healed the sick, one of the most holy and most venerated of the Dominicans in the Convent of Santo Stefano; of Brother Pedro, the Spaniard, and of Brother Domenico of Messina and Brother Giuseppe of Mussomeli. And they kept praising the virtues of Brother Vincenzo of Santo Stefano, of whom his fellow villagers had every reason to be proud: he had died just six months before Giacinto was born and was already worshiped as a blessed soul, in Palermo, in Santo Stefano, and in other places where he had spent his holy, industrious life and wherever his fame had spread. His was an example to follow.

Giacinto listened all agog to the tales of his virtues and miracles. And he prayed before his miraculous image, which was carried into the presence of the sick in order to heal them, and he prayed to the relics of the Saints; and he saw the plaits of women, and the wax molds that were taken to the altar of St Dominic by those who had received a blessing.

He enjoyed visiting all the churches in Santo Stefano; he often returned to the Mother Church, where he had been christened, and he was not yet seventeen when he stood godfather to a child christened at the same Font. He would return to the altars, kneeling with great fervor and admiring the ancient pictures; one very large one showed the village's three Patron Saints: St Stephen, the intrepid deacon who never hesitated to admonish his persecutors who resisted the Holy Spirit, and who was a Protomartyr of the Church; Our Lady of the Chain, the Most Holy Virgin who broke the chains of the prisoners locked up in the church on the Palermo seafront; and St Rosalia, who for the sake of her Lord Jesus Christ preferred a life of solitude and sacrifice in a freezing cave to all the privileges of the Norman court.

He too felt the call of God and resolved to be a priest of Christ: he begged the Dominican Fathers to allow him to become a Dominican too.

There was no lack of Dominican convents in the area; there was one in Bivona too, where they had celebrated the chapter the very year Giacinto was born. Bivona was close to Santo Stefano: one could walk there in an hour. But Bivona was not Santo Stefano; it was like another world. How many tragedies happened in that village! Depredations, profanations, violence of every kind! The signs were still there to be seen. Many folk in Santo Stefano believed that the inhabitants of Bivona did not fear God as they did: how many people from Bivona had been sentenced by the Holy Inquisition and condemned to the stake for heresy! It was a common subject of talk in Santo Stefano and many local people knew what it meant to be condemned by the Holy Inquisition, for they had seen the spectacular burnings in Palermo for the triumph of the Holy Faith.

When word spread of the public proclamations and the promised indulgences, many there were who would hasten — despite the distance and the dangers of the journey — to leave Santo Stefano, and the other towns, and make their way to the Bocceria, or Piazza Bologni, or the Ucciardone, or the Marina square, where the sentences were carried out. And they had seen the parades, the penitents with their *sambenito*, a humiliation to which any inhabitant of Santo Stefano would have preferred death; and with their own eyes they had seen the offenders being burned alive, or cardboard statues of them if the heretics could not be caught; and finally the ashes were scattered in the wind, like wheat chaff on the threshing-floor.

They had earned their indulgences and returned to the village deeply impressed, more resolved than ever not to change for all the gold in the world, to remain perfect Christians for ever. How could they forget what they had seen? They spoke of it all the time, they swore they would rather die than lose the grace of God. Everyone should be like the people of Santo Stefano — there would be no more people sentenced to the *sambenito*, the whip, the gag, or the stake.

But the people of Bivona were always being talked about! What about Stefano Cognata, who was hanged in Palermo? It was another matter in Bivona. That Bivona women were different from those of Santo Stefano was common knowledge. But even the monks in Bivona were not like those of Santo Stefano; there were some among them who misbehaved, like the young fellow that the people of Santo Stefano and Cammarata — everyone in fact — called the *priestling of Bivona*, who was a great source of concern for the Capuchin friars. For if the friars did not set the right example, who ever would?

The good Dominicans of Santo Stefano all agreed they should send Giacinto to Girgenti, to the novitiate house of the Province of Trinacria. And the boy left his village. He became accustomed to living far from home, but the name he chose for himself, Brother Giordano of Santo Stefano, was a constant promise, a pledge to recall — wherever he might be — not only the Blessed Jordan of Saxony, the first successor to St Dominic, but also the Protomartyr of the Church and his native village.

Girgenti was not a big city; it had just over ten thousand inhabitants. But its diocese was immense and everywhere, especially along the steep little lanes that wound their way up to the Cathedral of San Gerlando, one could often see monks and priests on their way to the Bishop's palace, to sort out some business or beg some favor. Many were the churches and convents of friars and monasteries in Girgenti. For centuries the Dominicans had had their convent there too; and for some years now they had been in the new one — a dozen friars could live there in comfort.

After the Sacred Council of Trent the bishops of Girgenti, as elsewhere, had committed themselves in every way to the renewal of Christian life, to the correction of people's ways, and to the eradication of sin: for this reason they would hold the Diocesan Synods. One they would always remember in particular was that celebrated in 1589 by the Spanish Monsignor Don Diego de Haedo, who had been Inquisitor in the kingdoms of Valencia and Aragon and then of Sicily. The king of Spain, Philip II, had made him Bishop of Girgenti and then Archbishop of Palermo, and to Palermo Don Diego had brought an arm of St Gerlando.

Everything was spelled out in the Synod Constitutions, which were laws for every part of the diocese and which everyone had to follow: on divine worship, the administration of the Sacraments, the Cathedral and its Chapter, the Holy Distribution, the sacristans, the Chapel Master, the Seminary, the lay Brotherhoods, the *Monti di Pietà* and the hospitals, the processions, the nuns, the diocesan visits, the Outlying Vicars, the life and morality of the clergy, the concubinaries and the intemperate, the moneylenders, sorcerers and blasphemers, burials and funerals, the court of law and punishments.

Parents had to baptize their children within three days of birth at the latest, but the same day was preferable. It was forbidden to let children sleep in the same bed as their wet-nurse lest they might suffocate. The curates were instructed not to allow children to be given pagan names: they had to be named after Saints. Whoever knew the name of the father or mother of a foundling child had to inform the Bishop or his Vicar so that the parents would be obliged to take the child back and nourish it. And whoever secretly took such a child to the hospice would be excommunicated and made to pay the wet-nurse for a year for the cost of feeding the child.

The curates had to tell the fathers and mothers of families not to let their sons sleep with their daughters after the age of ten years. They had to teach their children the ways of Christian life on Sundays after Vespers, *dato Campanæ signo* and after the sacristan had gathered them all together in the church at the sound of the bell: they had to direct them on the path to religion and the fear of God, to obedience and the respect of parents and priests.

The first thing that teachers from other towns had to do if they wanted to open a new school in Girgenti or elsewhere in the diocese was to place their profession of faith in the hands of the local Vicar, who would carefully examine their way of life, their customs, their manner of teaching, and the authors they read, for first and foremost it was their task to teach the Christian way of life. No teacher who aroused any suspicion could be allowed to exercise his profession, just as no woman could be a midwife if she could not baptize a child in case of need. In the schools it was not permitted to read pagan authors of fables *aut vana et discola tractantes*, even less so in the monasteries: books in the vulgar tongue that told of love and war, such as those of Petrarch and Ariosto, could not be kept, on pain of excommunication.

The minimum age for marriage, save by special licence of the Bishop, was fourteen years for males and twelve for females, but fourteen for female orphans married by members of the lay Brotherhoods, the Rectors being personally responsible for paying the dowry: for when a maiden was taken to her husband's house she had to be useful and a true help to the man. The curates were not to give their blessing to anyone wishing to marry who did not know the Hail Mary, the Lord's Prayer, or the Symbol of the Apostles. Heavy was the fine for those — and there were a few in Girgenti and several other parts of the diocese — who started sleeping together before the publications had been made and without receiving the curate's blessing, but only waiting for the dowry contract to be settled and the ring exchanged. And the parents would incur the same penalty if they permitted it.

If a married man, while his spouse was still alive, attempted to contract a second marriage, he would be condemned to be publicly whipped while wearing the miter of ignominy and then sent to the galleys for at least five years; a married woman would be whipped and sent into perpetual exile. And in both cases they would be obliged to respect the first marriage.

Confessors were expected to rebuke any women who, especially during Lent, went to confession wearing a tight dress or too much make-up, and, if they thought fit, they were to defer absolution until the next day. Nor were they to absolve those who, like moneylenders for example, would persist in not returning what they were unlawfully withholding or who would not at least give the injured party some assurance that he would regain possession of his belongings. If someone so instructed refused to return what was due, he would be excommunicated and denied church burial when he died. The curates were also enjoined to drive away from the church door any persons refusing to take the Sacrament of Penitence and to deny them Christian burial. Confessors were therefore obliged to write down the names and surnames of those whom they had confessed.

Anyone that knew of crimes or misdemeanors committed by priests, or of witches, enchantresses, procuresses or blasphemers, or of individuals who had testified falsely or committed incest, or of men who had two wives or women who had two husbands had to inform the Bishop or his representatives. The same obligation applied to those who knew of people who had not confessed or taken Holy Communion at Easter or had eaten meat, eggs, and dairy foods when this was forbidden. Or of pimps and usurers, or of illicit business, *sub pœna excommunicationis.* Nor could public notaries stipulate contracts involving usury or earnings that were in any way secret, under pain of returning their fee.

Whoever called the devil a saint or pronounced other blasphemies was to be reported to the Vicar or the Archpriest, so that he could be admonished; if the person persevered, he was to receive public punishment. If the blasphemy was not very serious, the penitent had to listen to Holy Mass being read on the day of a church festivity, in the main church, holding a lighted candle in his hands, while in the case of a person of low condition his tongue had to be pinched in front of the door of the church as Mass was being chanted.

Pimps were to be punished with a public whipping if the women they induced to sin were married; and if they were whores, with banishment from the town and the whole territory. The Bishop, at his discretion, could decide whether pimps were to be condemned to the trireme, and if a husband induced his own wife to sin, or a brother his sister, or a father his daughter, the man was to be condemned not only to the trireme but also to other punishments, always at the Bishop's discretion. The Vicar or the Archpriest or the Curate had to admonish the women, as discretely as possible, showing them the seriousness of their sin and the danger to which they were exposing themselves. And if a husband was acquiescent to his wife's committing adultery he was to be punished in the same manner and publicly whipped, and the woman could never see the adulterer again.

In certain cases, only the Bishop or his deputy could absolve the penitent: those who had committed murder and their instigators; those who had resorted to abortion; those who had committed incest of the first or second degree, or sacrilege with a nun, or sodomy, or bestiality, or who had raped a virgin; or who had committed perjury with damage to the offended party or committed the crime of simony; or who had refused to pay their tithes within the year or give their first-fruits or pay their debts to monasteries, churches, hospitals, and *Monti di Pietà*, or respect the terms of legacies for religious purposes, etc.

Physicians had to be persuaded that above all it was the soul of the sick that had to be healed, as the infirmity of the body was often caused by sin. Therefore, on pain of excommunication, the physician on his second visit had to persuade the patient to confess and take communion, and if the next time the patient did not present a certificate of confession, he was no longer to go and treat the patient, but instead inform the Bishop. Doctors also had to urge their patients to write their will and to leave instructions for the apportioning of their belongings.

Hired female mourners, on pain of whipping, were to refrain from their wailing in the house of the dead. Sacristans were not to strip bodies of their clothes and belongings, on pain of excommunication and other punishments laid down in the Sacred Canons, *ipso facto*.

Men and women were not to mix in any church where the Holy Eucharist was being administered: they were to take Communion at two separate altars. *Sub pœna excommunicationis*, laymen could not sit in the stalls of the Choir reserved for priests and ecclesiastics. Believers were not to eat at the same table with non-believers or sleep in the same bed.

When the Most Holy Eucharist was taken to the sick, all those who saw it go by, on pain of excommunication, had to kneel on both knees, uncover their head, and dismount if on horseback. All priests and churchmen, and monks of every order, had to wear a short surplice, *sub pœna interdicti*, during the celebrations for *Corpus Domini*. The Brotherhoods of laymen had to attend all processions and the brethren had to wear their habit and walk with their face covered and the Crown in their hands, reciting their prayers. Unless the Pope had approved, churchmen or others who had recently died could not be revered as Saints, even if their merits might make them appear worthy of it.

All those who had taken holy orders had to go their rounds wearing the cloth, on pain of suspension for one week from the portions of the Holy Distribution. In order that laymen and the ministers of civil justice in particular should no longer treat churchmen with violence, with the excuse they could not recognize them, the Bishop ordered that all those who had taken holy orders, including seminarists, even if only tonsured, were to wear the clerical cap and were not to grow their hair or a moustache or a beard, and when in church or in town or indeed anywhere they were to wear a black cassock, and never colored shoes or other garments, but only black or dark or gray. Nor could priests wear garments of silk or cloth lined with silk, except around the neck, or white stockings or shirts with frills around the neck or wrists, or use perfumes. If those belonging to the minor orders could not, through poverty, afford a full-length cassock, they were at least to wear the short black sort that reached to the knee, on pain of two weeks' imprisonment. Those who instead belonged to the major orders could wear the short cassock that reached down to the knee only when in the country, as also the non-conical-shaped biretta and cloak; they were however obliged to don the regular clerical biretta when in church or in the Bishop's palace when they wished to be admitted to his presence.

Brother Giordano learned many things in Girgenti. Now his home was the Dominican convent in that town; there he spent the year of his novitiate and made his vows. In this convent they often spoke of the missionaries who departed from Spain on their way to the Far East; the *barcadas* mostly sailed from Seville for New Spain, whence they proceeded to the Philippines and from the Philippines to Japan. Many indeed were the Spaniards in Girgenti and some very important positions and charges they had; there were some in the convents too, in the churches, and in the Bishop's palace: Don John Oroczo de Cavarrubias was another Spaniard, and he too had been made a bishop by Philip II. Now Don Vincenzo Bonincontro, one of Cardinal Borghese's theologians, was bishop: he had celebrated another Synod and wanted to turn the Seminary in Girgenti into a major center of training and culture.

But everywhere in Sicily one could breathe the air of Spain. Palermo, the Kingdom's capital, had every appearance of a Spanish town: one could admire the magnificence of the Viceroys, of the most powerful noblemen, of the Archbishop and the inflexible Inquisitors, and everywhere one would meet Spaniards, even common folk, but always proud of Spain and her king, the Catholic King. Many convents, churches, houses, and squares were like those in Madrid, Valencia, and Seville. The Dominicans had two convents there, San Domenico and Santa Zita, and many went to and fro between Palermo and Spain: Father Pietro Cannizzaro, the Provincial of Sicily, had studied in Valencia too, under the guide of the holy missionary Ludovico Bertrando, and he always spoke with fiery words of missionaries and far-away lands where there was great need of such men.

Increasingly, Brother Giordano wanted to be in God's service, a priest and a missionary; he wanted to go to Spain to continue his studies and to prepare himself, to have the opportunity and the good fortune to leave one day in order to go and preach the faith of Christ in the lands of the infidel. His superiors noted his exceptional capacities, his intelligence and his particular missionary vocation, his mountain-dweller's determined resoluteness; they listened to his prayers. Spain needed men like him.

And so Brother Giordano returned to Santo Stefano to get what was strictly necessary: to ask the blessing of the good Fathers of the convent who had opened the doors to receive him into the Dominican family, and to salute his relatives, his childhood companions, all the people of his village. For journeys were very dangerous, as everyone knew; indeed it was standard practice to settle one's affairs and write one's will even before journeying to Naples or Rome. He was leaving on a longer journey and he could not tell if he would ever return.

And so once again he left his town. As he walked away, he gazed at the houses, the bell-towers of the Mother Church and the Church of San Domenico, the fields with the farms and the haystacks, his mountains; the grass changing color, the stones, and the cottages that looked like grazing goats and sheep.

Farewell, crystal springs and streams and plashing rivers, farewell sweet-smelling woods; farewell Muntivernu, Margimutu, Quisquina; farewell, Pizzo di San Calò.

For as long as he could, he tried to pick out the mountaintop, just as he had always done since his earliest childhood. He continued to think of his mother and father, of his little brothers that he had never known, of his ancestors, buried in the churches beneath the mountain, and he prayed for them; he bore them all in his heart. Then even the little church of San Calò disappeared.

IV.
Even the Spaniards Came to Love Him

Going to Spain was a privilege. There were famous centers of Christian spiritual and cultural training there, and Sicilians who were lucky enough to set foot there were welcomed and respected as if they were Spaniards themselves. They became like them, there was no division between dominators and the dominated. Everyone was favored and protected by the Catholic King. Various Sicilians had been trained in Valencia, under the guidance of the holy missionary Ludovico Bertrando: every Dominican knew who he was.

Brother Giordano had had the good fortune to be assigned to the Convent of Saint Stephen at Salamanca, one of the most famous cultural centers in the world, indeed so famous that it was said that if you did not become a scholar at Salamanca, it meant that you were a real dullard, that nature had not given you the ability to learn, and that therefore there was nothing to be done. The Dominicans of Salamanca were proud men, even haughty, because of their cultural traditions and because people listened to them wherever they went, at Court and even in the New World. Every Dominican, all over the world, wanted to go to Salamanca, even for just a short time. Those who were lucky enough to get there wanted to stay forever. But in order to go, there had to be a fully justified proposal by the Provincial Chapter, and the General of the Order had the final word. Only friars who showed uncommon ability were sent to Salamanca.

Brother Giordano had shown he was exceptionally quick at learning — this he showed in the rapid progress he made in learning Greek and Latin. Now he could continue his studies in philosophy and theology, extend his knowledge of the peoples of the East, and learn more of the life of a missionary in those faraway lands, as he could speak to members of his confraternity who had visited them. His desire to travel became even more burning and he made a formal request to the Father Provincial of Spain. The Father did not doubt the qualities of the young man from Santo Stefano, his intelligence, his earnestness, and the seriousness of his intentions, and he assigned him to the convent of Trujillo in Castile.

Trujillo was in the diocese of Placencia and in the province of Cáceres, near the border with Portugal. It could boast the glories of conquest: various explorers of the New World had left from there, including Francisco Pizarro, the *conquistador* of Peru. But Trujillo was also an austere center for the training of missionaries, who had to curb the violence of the conquerors and carry the Gospel far and wide. The Dominican Convent of the Incarnation was there. In this convent Brother Giordano extended his studies still further and continued to prepare for his great journey. He was immediately loved both in the convent and in the town for his intelligence and presence of mind, his natural modesty, his kindness and good manners. He also started to carry out his mission as a priest and despite his young age many people came looking for him and wanted him as their spiritual father, listening to his words with devoted attention. His chastity was also exemplary: he did not look at women and avoided talking to them.

Father John of Saint Paul happened to pass through Trujillo. This man was an intrepid missionary who had had spent many years in the Philippines. He was always urging the members of his confraternity to leave for the Far East, where there was great need of God's workers. Brother Giordano listened to his tales with amazement; his words were like sparks inflaming the young man's soul and, as he later said, they seemed to him to be a letter sent by God to show him what he was to do in His service. Father John told of the relentless persecutions taking place in Japan, of the desire of many Japanese people to learn God's word and be converted, of the lack of priests to teach them the Holy Faith, and of the strength with which the converted suffered martyrdom because of their faith. That was when Brother Giordano felt the flame of divine love and decided he could wait no longer to leave for Japan to preach the word of salvation and give his life to Jesus Christ. The name of Saint Francis Xavier was then on everyone's lips, the great Spanish Jesuit, the companion of Saint Ignatius of Loyola and the evangelizer of India, Japan, and China, who had been beatified in 1619 and canonized three years later.

But leaving for the East was no everyday matter — it required more than the desire of the missionaries and the permission of their superiors. No Dominican had left Spain for the Philippines since 1620. An authorization was required from the Catholic King, as well as permission from the superiors of the Order.

Finally, in 1625, Philip IV gave his permission for a new expedition, or *barcada*, as it was called in Spanish, with funds for twenty Dominicans. This seemed to Brother Giordano to be another sign of God's will: it was his moment, when would he have another similar opportunity? With all his might, but always with great humility, he begged his superiors to let him be one of the twenty; his wish was granted.

Everyone knew with what rigor the friars were chosen for missions and everyone congratulated Brother Giordano and repeated to him that it was God's will. Friars who wished to go and preach the Holy Gospel to the infidels in the Philippine Islands and in China were obliged to read and sign a paper that clearly set out what they were in for. The paper first listed the difficulties of the journey from Spain to New Spain, which lasted three and a half months and sometimes even four. It was very hard because of the heat, the rotting food supplies, hunger, and the dirty conditions on board ship. After disembarking, they had to walk the seventy leagues to Mexico City. This too was difficult, with many risks to the health. From Mexico City they had to walk the same distance again to Acapulco and then face another long and dangerous sea crossing, which lasted at least two and a half months. Once in the Philippine Islands, they had to adapt to conditions there as best they could, sometimes even living in caves. After being assigned to the mission, they had to learn the local language — no easy task — in order to be able to communicate with the infidels and catechize them. In the administration of the Sacraments, they had to follow the formulary they had been given in New Spain. Whenever the Bishop decided to establish clergy in the town they happened to be in, the friars had to leave and preach elsewhere. They could not stay long in the same place in this life. Their main task was to convert the infidels, and their life was one of continuous penance and prayer. They were expected to set an example of holiness. The first thing they had to do was to conform to the rigor of the Sacred Constitutions *ut iacet*. They had to read them frequently and correct and accuse each other in their daily meetings. Secondly, they had to be poor. They could not have any belongings, whether communal or personal. They were all expected to live in the community and follow the same rules. Thirdly, they had to wear rough sackcloth or other coarse garments; they were allowed to build only very poor houses for themselves, not large and expensive ones; and they could not keep precious objects in their cells and in the common areas, only modest church furnishings. Fourthly, they had to go everywhere on foot, observe silence and abstinence, sleep without mattresses on bare wooden boards using just a mat and a blanket, and mortify their bodies every night according to the rules of the community, as was the custom in Spanish convents. In all things they did, they had to conform to the practices of the Founding Fathers of Mexico and Chiapa in order to convert the Indios. Also, each day, they had to read something from the lives of the Saints, and in all their conversation, amongst themselves and with others, they had to speak of God and of the things that bring one to God, severely condemning any other subject of speech.

Brother Giordano accepted all this with joy. It was exactly what he wanted and he wanted to do even more. He felt that God had answered his prayers. But even amid such joy, his heart was still tormented, humble as he was: he could not see how he could ever accomplish such a noble mission, though his desire to suffer and die for Christ was none the less sincere and great. He prayed and prayed and his determination to leave became even greater: but if he was not chosen for the mission like the other fathers, he could still serve them.

The departure was coming closer and, as often happens when one is about to do something new, Brother Giordano could not help thinking back to what his life had been until then. He thought of the town where he was born and where his parents were buried, and it seemed ever further away. And yet a message had arrived all the way to Spain from that remote mountain village. The inhabitants had witnessed extraordinary events and the news had spread everywhere. Many spoke now of Santo Stefano, even if they had no idea where it was or what it was like.

Two builders from Palermo were constructing a new Dominican convent right in the middle of Santo Stefano. With some local people they had gone to Quisquina, where they discovered the grotto of Saint Rosalia and an inscription about the life she had chosen to live, which the Saint herself had carved in the hard stone of the cave. All this had happened in August 1624, a month after the bones of the Hermit Saint had been found on Mount Pellegrino. Hopes were raised once again that Palermo might be rid of the plague that was tormenting the city. Everyone wanted fragments of the miraculous relics, but the City Senators decided it was only right and proper to send them to their king, the Catholic King. So it was that Philip IV and many Spaniards first heard of the Hermit Saint of Quisquina, to whom they soon devoted themselves. The Dominican friars must certainly have asked Brother Giordano about his hometown and about Quisquina. Many of them had probably never heard of the town before, even though one of their most illustrious brethren, Brother Tommaso Fazello, the historian of Sicily, had written of a gold-mine on Mount Contubernio, above the town of Santo Stefano, and of a saltwater spring and an oil-well, as also of the Mount of Roses on the slopes of Mount Quisquina, which was famous for its miraculous herbs. Herbalists and other people came from all over to gather these herbs, which were used to cure both people and animals.

Brother Giordano was far away from Quisquina. He could not see or live the experience of those extraordinary events alongside his brethren and his fellow townsmen, events that took place on the eve of his departure on his most noble mission.

Many are the ways to serve Our Lord! Saint Rosalia had left the luxury of the Palermo court and renounced a life of comfort, to seek a life of complete solitude. She had hidden first in a cave at Quisquina and later in a cave on Mount Pellegrino, in order to be closer to God. She had lived in places which Giacinto had known since he was a little boy and which he had left in order to become a servant of Christ. The humility, determination, sacrifices, and penance of that fragile woman were an example to him. She was the daughter of Sinibaldi, lord of Quisquina and of the Roses. Giordano too came from an illustrious family, the Ansalones, formerly lords of Santo Stefano, but rather than a hermit's life he had chosen that of a missionary, of a man who goes among the people and faces their threats, their deceits, and their persecution, but always serves his God, and like Saint Rosalia he was bound to remain faithful to his choice.

The moment arrived. Brother Giordano tearfully bade farewell to his superiors, to his brethren and friends, and to the congregation of Trujillo, who had become fond of him. He set off on foot for Seville, begging for alms. He walked for many days, mostly in desert areas, through thorns and under a relentless sun. He walked until he was exhausted by fatigue, thirst, and the anxiety of arriving in good time, without wasting a moment of the life God had granted him. And every day he awoke in that almost African landscape with renewed strength and happily resumed his journey, never ceasing to praise his God.

He saw the tower of Giralda high in the blue of the sky and he finally arrived in Seville, where he rejoined his companions. It was baking in the city and many people were bathing in the Guadalquivir, which was full of boats. There was a great bustling to and fro, with multitudes of people in the port, of all different races. Some bore brand marks upon their cheek or nose: they were slaves who were bought and sold like animals. Nor were they treated much better than animals, which were branded on the ears, the neck, or the flanks.

The friars waited all together until the moment they were to embark. They were much struck by what they saw. Finally they started off, that same year, under the leadership of Father Hyacinth Calvo, Procurator of the Missions of the Province of the Philippines in Madrid.

V.
Jordanus Non Est Conversus Retrorsum

During the journey Brother Giordano continued his charity work, taking care of those who were sick, encouraging those who felt disheartened, constantly speaking of the missionaries' duties, of God, and of His commandments, and doing his utmost to make himself useful. He enjoyed conversing with Brother Hyacinth of the Rosary, who like him aspired to take the word of God to Japan and, for this reason, wanted to learn the language and the traditions of the people of the East; they both spent part of their time, whatever moments they could spare, studying on their own. To ordinary lay people they spoke no more than charity imposed, avoiding all useless chatter and vanities.

And so they crossed the Atlantic and landed in the harbor of Vera Cruz. Once again, Brother Giordano and his companions had to face a long, hard journey, all on foot. They saw the sinister pyramids of the Sun and the Moon and they felt immense sadness: the sooner the missionaries arrived the more victims could be spared! They arrived in Mexico City, at the Hospice of Saint Hyacinth, which the Province of the Philippines had founded outside the city walls in an area full of gardens, where the missionaries were able to rest and prepare for their further travels.

There were Spaniards even in those immense and distant lands, conquered by Cortés. When he arrived, he was shocked to see, in many places, human bodies with no legs or arms or other members, all bitten off, and to hear that other men had eaten them: the poor victims had been sacrificed to a god who demanded human blood, as the native Indians still believed, a god to whom they offered man's most vital part, the heart, torn still beating from the chest, which was ripped open with an obsidian knife. The best thing the conquistador did was to prohibit these human sacrifices, as well as cannibalism, which according to the sages of Salamanca would alone have justified the Spanish war of conquest.

How different Sicily was! There was, it is true, no lack in Sicily of macabre scenes: one could see the quarters of the executed at the top of roads and hanging on trees in the countryside, and heads and hands in cages on the walls of stately palaces. But they belonged to criminals and traitors, not innocent people. Two thousand years before, in 480 BC, one of the tyrants of Syracuse, Gelon, having defeated the Carthaginians with the help of his son-in-law Theron of Agrigento, imposed as a condition of the peace treaty that they should no longer sacrifice their children to the god Baal.

But Cortés was no saint either; he too had committed atrocities. Of this the Dominicans were well aware and they had accordingly protested: once, having foiled a plot, he sentenced some men to the gallows and one to have his feet cut off: he also had the informers' hands cut off at Tlaxcala.

In the Hospice of Saint Hyacinth stories were told of the doings of both conquistadors and missionaries. Cortés had arrived in Mexico with a priest from Seville and a Mercedarian friar, Brother Bartolomé, a man who sowed many a seed. He died comforted by the knowledge he had baptized some two thousand five hundred native Indians. Soon after, the Franciscans arrived and Emperor Charles V chose a Franciscan to be the first bishop of New Spain.

The atrocities the Spaniards committed could not be concealed. They proclaimed themselves to be devout Christians yet they behaved worse than the Turks. They exterminated the native Indians in New Spain and butchered them even when they surrendered unconditionally. They killed them even when they had welcomed them into their homes and given them all their belongings. How many they had beheaded, put to the sword, and burned alive, including old people, women, and children! Once Montezuma's brother and numerous great lords were sent by the king two leagues outside Mexico City to meet the Spaniards, along the wide road between the waters. They brought with them gifts of gold and silver as well as precious garments. Montezuma himself welcomed them at the gates of the city with his entire court and escorted them to his palace as his guests. And how did the Spaniards reward him? They took him prisoner and slaughtered all the nobles and ordinary citizens who were dancing in the streets to comfort their imprisoned king.

A friar recalled with horror how one of the Spaniards — who yet were Christians and indeed proud of it — once went hunting but, not finding any deer or rabbits to feed to his dogs, without a moment's hesitation seized a baby from its mother's breast, cut off its little arms and legs, and threw them to his hungry beasts, after which he tossed them the mutilated body.

Those who were left alive had to suffer continuous violence, pay tribute, and undergo every sort of hardship. The Spaniards used them as carriers, like mules, for the hardest labor. They made them work in the fields without any pay and sometimes did not even give them anything to eat or enough to survive on — often the Indians fell to the ground and died of hunger.

Most of the Spaniards were convinced that the native population were not human beings like the Christians and like themselves. Many learned scholars strove to prove that some people were superior to others in terms of intelligence and virtue, and these people were of course the Spaniards. The humanist Juan Ginés de Sepúlveda expressed the opinion that the native people were slaves by nature, half-men, barbarians, lechers, and cannibals. To his mind, they had neither humanity nor culture nor laws, as opposed to the Spaniards, who were prudent, intelligent, magnanimous, temperate, humane, and supremely religious. This humanist related how the natives, before the Christians' arrival, did not live in the peace of the mythical age of Saturn but continuously waged war with each other and would not be satisfied or consider themselves victorious until they appeased their hunger with their enemies' flesh, while these same men, at the sight of a handful of Spaniards, had shown what abject cowards they really were by running away like silly women. And what had the Mexicans done when faced by Cortés, those Mexicans who considered themselves and were considered the most civilized, intelligent, and courageous of men? They had shown their lazy, idle, coarse nature by doing nothing to free their king Montezuma from jail.

But after a while the Indians got to know the Spaniards better and realized they had not come down from heaven. They became more cautious and welcomed the Franciscans as long as they did not bring those cruel Christians with them. The friars gave their word and were immediately allowed to start preaching God's word. There were mass conversions of Indians, who brought their idols to the missionaries to be burned and their children to be taught the ways of the new religion. But the Spaniards started coming with idols they had taken from Indians in other areas and they would use force and threats to sell them – for each idol they demanded an Indian man or woman, who was then sold on to slave traders.

The people complained to the missionaries: "What! They want to sell us idols from other lands, after you have burned ours!" What about all the promises? The poor friars had nothing to do with it, but these evil plunderers convinced the native people that they had been called by the missionaries.

As a result the Indians decided to kill the Franciscans. But some were still faithful and warned the friars and they managed to escape. The Indians were sorry, for they had become fond of the friars. They soon repented and convinced themselves the missionaries were innocent, and went looking for them to seek their forgiveness. They begged the Franciscans to return among them and the missionaries decided to go back. However, despite all their pleas, these accursed plunderers would not leave and they continued to torment the native population. They even molested the missionaries, who refused to become their accomplices and eventually, fearing fresh revolts, left New Spain entirely.

The friars remembered what happened to the first Dominicans who went to the New World to preach God's word. The Indians welcomed them and listened to what they had to say, following their gestures, as they did not know the local language. But, as usual, the Spaniards arrived, like hawks, and took the Indians to sell as slaves. Those who were left behind, especially the relatives of the unlucky ones who had been taken away, asked the Dominicans the reason for all this. They had placed all their hopes in the missionaries and now they felt betrayed. The good friars tried to make amends as best they could and attempted to free the poor Indians. But as they did not succeed, they became the victims of the natives' revenge and were martyred.

Many other missionaries were killed. Even Brother Bartolomé de las Casas, who had always been on the Indians' side, only narrowly escaped death. More often than not, the natives did not understand the difference between the missionaries and the Spanish predators. Ever since the conquistadors had begun their conquests, the missionaries had annoyed them because they preached God's word and protested against the Spanish atrocities and the cruel way the Indians were treated. The friars opposed all those who believed in slavery and war on people who were not Christians. The friars repeated again and again that the Indians were God's children and that Jesus had died for them too. In impassioned language the Dominican Antonio de Montesinos condemned the cruelty of the Spanish colonizers of Hispaniola, and many other Dominicans sided with the oppressed. In particular Brother Bartolomé de las Casas, who had been bishop of Chiapa, denounced the atrocities committed by the Spanish soldiers and ministers. He showed that the Indians were in no way inferior to the Europeans, that they were men and women just as they themselves were, and that could be converted without the use of violence. Indeed, violence was contrary to religion. He declared that all the wars the Spaniards had waged on the Indians had been unjust, and that everything the Spaniards owned in the Indies was the fruit of robbery and should therefore be returned. He denied the Sacraments to all those who kept slaves. In the end his words reached the Spanish Court and were heeded. And so it was that slavery of the Indians was prohibited.

Brother Giordano was saddened to hear all these things and felt even more he was on the side of the oppressed. He felt he had to give them all his love and try to put right other people's wrongs, as far as that was within his power. The Spaniards in Spain and also in Sicily, for example in Santo Stefano or Girgenti, did not seem so cruel. Why did such things happen in New Spain? Perhaps because it was so far away from Spain? Were the Spaniards' hands less tied there, so that they let their most brutal instincts run free? The Catholic King could not be aware of everything his ministers and soldiers did in his name.

New Spain belonged to the King of Spain, as did Sicily. However, the Mexicans were not in the same conditions as the Sicilians. Even in that distant land many people spoke Spanish, as did people in Sicily. They prayed to the same Saints, and numerous Mexicans had even become missionaries and wanted to go to Japan to preach the Gospel. There were the spectacles prepared by the Holy Inquisition, and autos-da-fé were celebrated in the Church of St Dominic in Mexico City, just as they were in the Church of San Domenico in the capital of Sicily. And there were solemn processions, magnificent parades, and bullfights, which threw the Mexicans into raptures — the Sicilians, on the contrary, did not care much for them.

There were many races in New Spain: the native Indians, blacks, Creoles, mulattos, Zambos, and Europeans. There were also many people who might have been taken for Sicilians, from Girgenti — they had the same faces, which quite amazed the missionaries! Many things in that distant world recalled Spain, and Brother Giordano could not help thinking about Sicily. The sky, the prickly pears, the fields of cereal crops, and many other plants were the same. Cortés had been right to name this colony New Spain. The friars could scarcely believe they had come so far, and indeed some died during the journey or soon after their arrival.

The missionaries stayed in the Hospice of St Hyacinth for several months. They spent their days there and rarely went into town, and then only when they had some task to perform. They prayed, did penance, preached God's word, and experienced the joy of converting many Indians to their religion and baptizing them.

Brother Giordano also had other thoughts on his mind: he wanted to learn new things and write them down in order to let everyone else share the fruits of his studies. Whenever he could, he would get away from his companions and spend some time alone. He wrote an elegant summary in Latin of the *Lives* of the Dominican Saints, which had been written in Spanish by Brother Hernando del Castillo. Never idle, he continued to work even on days that were meant for rest.

In the meantime, the day for his new journey was getting closer. The friars' superiors and companions did not hide from them anything of what they could expect. The guides and the instructions, which they read over and over again, were very clear. In 1586, in the Convent of St Dominic in Mexico City, the Vicar General Brother John de Castro had dictated the General Orders for the new province of the Most Holy Rosary. The missionaries had to behave as they themselves had to teach — in other words they had to practice what they preached. Men who were expected to guide others along the path of perfection had to lead the way, just as Jesus Christ had done, who acted before preaching and did good deeds before teaching others to do them. They were expected to save their own soul before that of others. What is the good of gaining the whole world if a man forfeits his soul and is damned? Good teaching converts the infidels more effectively if combined with honest living. So that the holy life of Jesus Christ should be manifest through them, the missionaries continuously had to mortify their bodies with acts of penitence and fasting. They had a narrow path to follow and were expected to abide not only by the essential rules, such as the Holy Commandments and their vows, but also by the non-essential rules. Thus they had to follow the particular Constitutions most rigorously – they had to fast, eat fish rather than meat, wear coarse and humble woollen clothes, observe silence, and walk rather than ride horseback. Everything was expected to be in uniform style, for example the quantity and quality of their garments, the religious ceremonies, and the celebration of Holy Mass. All churches had to be the same, all opinions, all decisions; all doctrines had to conform, as well as the administering of the Holy Sacraments. All conversation had to be spiritual, and everyone was expected to speak as if with one mouth and to avoid all differences. There was supposed to be unity in the worship of God, in one mouth, one sentiment, and one concept.

Night and day the missionaries had to recite all the Hours in church, even if they were few in number, and they had to get up at midnight. Whenever one of the missionaries died, each friar had to celebrate six masses, *in solidum*, whilst those who were not missionaries had to recite the Psalms and the Rosary. They were expected to put a stop to profane talk, forestall all novelty, and shun idle words. In order to inflame their love of the divine, they constantly read the Fathers, ecclesiastical histories, the Holy Scriptures, and the relevant commentaries. And as the Bishops were the Shepherds of their flock, the first thing the missionaries had to do when they arrived in a new diocese was to visit the Bishop. After receiving his blessing, they would preach as he advised them and show him obedience for as long as they stayed in his diocese. They were expected to renounce their own will in order to follow that of their Father Superior, both in their assignment and in their preaching. They had to avoid visits to lay persons, unless made for charity's sake and with their Superior's authorization. And if it was necessary to ask for charity, only the Superior could select the person to do so. What joy to be utterly poor! The convent buildings had to be humble too. Expenses were kept to a bare minimum and in the cells there could be nothing that suggested pomp or anything contrary to poverty. Friars could keep only one holy image and that had to be plain and without decoration. This applied to everyone, from the Superiors down to simple friars. In Manila, the Father Provincial Brother Alonso Jiménez was found to be using a marked spoon, but no exception was made for him: in the Provincial Chapter of 1594 it was established, according to the principle of uniformity, that no missionary could carry on his person or use at table any personal objects, such as bowls and spoons. Any books or objects that the friars might acquire belonged to the Province of the Most Holy Rosary.

The friars spent two hours a day in silent prayer and divine contemplation, whether they were in the convent or elsewhere. On days when there was no Office of Our Lady, they had to recite the Psalms and antiphons in Her honor. Every day, except on Sundays, major festivities, and the solemn octave, they mortified their bodies with a scourge. They slept on a wooden board without a mattress, with just a palm mat and two blankets.

These Ordinances were solemnly read out to the missionaries before they left New Spain; and they were expected to continue to observe them. If they felt they could not, they could return to Spain, for one discontented friar would do more harm than good and would only dishearten many others — and this was, as they knew, a very contagious malady. The friars were thus left to make their own choice because only those who volunteered to go could be expected to serve God joyfully. Some missionaries had arrived in Mexico City, weary after their long and perilous journey and fearful of new dangers, and finding that New Spain was a safe land that reminded them of Spain they remained there or returned later to Europe. Numerous Dominicans had been punished by being sent from New Spain to the Philippines, for example Brother John Cobo and Brother Luis Gandullo, who were expelled by the Viceroy for preaching against public scandals in which he himself was accused of being involved.

The day of departure was coming close and not even these brave missionaries could help thinking of the dangers ahead and what had happened to many friars who had gone before them. They also thought of their families and of other people who needed them. One in particular felt tempted to return to Spain and he asked Brother Giordano if he too had thought of going back.

"*Jordanus non est conversus retrorsum,*" replied the resolute friar from the mountains of Santo Stefano: he was not the Jordan that turned back — he was determined to see through what he had started, even if it were to cost him his life.

And so it was that Brother Giordano and his companions set out on foot from the Hospice of St Hyacinth and started the long, hard march to the port of Acapulco, on the Pacific coast. They knew of the extreme heat they would encounter on the way and realized that not everyone would survive it. Even the name of the place inspired fear — Acapulco, the Mouth of Hell.

They set sail on 26 March 1626. Their leader was Father Alonso Sánchez of the Visitation, Vicar of St Hyacinth, appointed Commissioner for the Province of New Segovia by the Mexican Inquisition. The friars resumed the charitable acts to which they had devoted their energies during their last voyage. After many months at sea, they finally reached Manila.

VI.
The Missionary Center in Manila

The Spaniards had gone as far as the Philippines, naming the islands in honor of their king, Philip II. Miguel López de Legazpi had occupied them in 1565. In 1571 a fortress had been built on the island of Luzon, in Manila, which was to be the new colony's capital. In accordance with the express desire of the Dominicans, the Catholic King had ordered the conquistador not to perpetrate acts of violence or injustice of any kind. And the conquistador, being a God-fearing man, listened to the words of the Augustinian father Andrés de Urdaneta, who knew the Philippines well.

But the Spaniards did not follow their instructions and showed the worst side of their nature, as they had in other places. They imposed the payment of heavy tributes on the natives. They were greedy, constantly wanting more and more money, more merchandise, and more work out of the men. In exchange, they promised to protect them and to help them become good Christians, according to the Catholic King's wishes. The Philippines were to become a great Catholic haven in the immense pagan world, and from there the light of the Holy Faith was to spread to other lands.

The missionaries accompanying the Spanish soldiers thus had to persuade the natives to submit to the king of Spain. In reward they would receive the dual grace of civilization and Christianity. For this purpose, the Augustines and then the Franciscans, the Dominicans, the Jesuits, and the Recollects had all come to the islands. The Dominican province of the Most Holy Rosary of the Philippines was founded after the arrival in 1587 of fifteen friars led by Father Juan de Castro. Its purpose was to convert the infidels.

It was not easy for the Spaniards to hold on to Manila and the archipelago. The Dutch and the British steadfastly opposed their domination, causing such serious losses that at one point King Philip IV became disheartened and almost abandoned the islands to their destiny. But what would then have been the point of all the *barcadas* and all the sacrifices of so many soldiers and missionaries who had tried to turn the islanders into good Christians? He thus decided to stand by the islands, whatever the cost — after all, did not he too bear the glorious title of Catholic King! The natives took sides with the Spaniards, against the other Europeans. They looked upon the enemies of Spain as their own enemies, as had happened in other parts of the empire, including Sicily.

But the missionaries who had spread throughout the many islands wanted the Filipinos to be fairly treated. They were against the arrogance of the colonizers, who really wanted to turn the people into slaves, more like animals than people. Even the monks required the labor of those they had converted, but for different purposes. They wanted them to build their churches and perform other labors that would serve their specific needs and the general good. The missionaries knew they should always treat the Indios with great love and charity, not only in theory but also in practice. They knew they should try to meet their needs and, if punishment was really necessary, others were to mete it out, for the Indios were to receive only good from their hands. In this way they would become attached to the law that the missionaries preached.

There had always been trade between the islands and China. Many Chinese had settled in Luzon, forming a large quarter outside Manila. They were different from everybody else as they had the special virtue of being able to adapt to any job: they were artisans, laborers, market gardeners, bakers, porters, and boatmen. The name of China inspired respect. Many merchants arrived from China bringing luxury items, silks, porcelain, and gold, as well as furniture, iron tools, dyes, and animals. They exchanged everything for the silver that the Spanish galleons brought from New Spain. As well as active men, there were also disabled and sick people, beggars, and outcasts.

Here in Manila, the Dominicans had immediately resolved to convert these Chinese, of whatever condition, who lived in the Parian colony by the city walls. There they founded a hospital, the Hospital of St Gabriel, as that was what was most needed. The village of Binondo was established on the other side of the Pasig river, and the Christian Chinese went to live there — the hospital was also transferred there. In the meantime a new and larger hospital was completed, in 1625, but it was not big enough for all the sick. It was always full and the missionaries kept on converting the patients.

They managed to win over and baptize nearly all the infidels who entered the hospital, thanks to their virtues and their sacrifices, which were without either personal interest or worldly reward. The Dominicans also founded the College of Saint Thomas, which received official authorization to confer academic degrees.

Not far from the Parian colony was that of the Japanese. The islands had always aroused the interest of these Japanese, who had more than once threatened Manila with arms.

Manila was thus a great city. It was rich, thanks to its port, and safe because the sea and the great river surrounded it on all sides, lapping its walls. It was the capital of the Philippines and the seat of the Governor and General Captain, of the Audience Chamber, and of the Royal Chancellery. The chief military garrison was stationed there and on it depended all the forces that watched over all the islands. Manila lacked nothing — goods of every kind arrived from every corner, including wheat, so that the Spaniards could have the same bread as they had in Spain, while other people ate rice. Bread was even served in the convent refectories, although many of the missionaries renounced it out of humility and as a penance, eating rice instead, because here rice was the local bread and should be the same for everybody.

VII.
The Miraculous Image of Our Lady of the Rosary

Brother Giordano from Santo Stefano was also in Manila now, one of the Fathers of the Province of the Most Holy Rosary. Some twenty years had gone by since he had started attending the Dominican convent in his remote village of Santo Stefano, which shared the same name. So many convents, churches, and confraternities were dedicated to the Most Holy Rosary! — propagated by the Patriarch Saint Dominic the ever victorious, the terror of heresies, the comfort and guide of Christopher Columbus in his adventurous voyage towards the unknown, the triumpher at Lepanto!

In the convent in Manila, in the Chapel of the Rosary, there was a miraculous image of extraordinary beauty of Our Lady of the Rosary. The face and hands were made of ivory, as was the Child. The image, done by a Chinaman, had been commissioned by Don Luis Pérez Dasmariñas, Governor of the Philippines, who was utterly devoted to the Dominicans and had donated it to the convent. All the faithful wanted an image like this one and many people went to the best artists, ready to pay any sum of money. But nobody succeeded in producing an image anything like it.

"This Lady does not want her portrait done," the artists would say, as one by one they gave up the task. The Chinese painter was a heathen and he had wanted to be baptized in front of the image he had made.

The image stood on a beautiful throne with a precious gold retablo. In the chapel were fourteen silver lamps and forty-two candlesticks, twenty of which were very large. There were also two great silver candelabra with twelve candlesticks and a precious lamp. The chapel was full of jewels that had been offered by those who had received acts of grace. Outside the chapel (there was no room inside) there were numerous boards on which the miracle scenes had been painted, including that of the miracle of 1613, the most famous of all.

One day, Lady Anna de Vera, a woman who regularly dressed the sacred image and changed its clothes according to the day and the festivities, was on her way to the chapel together with a group of other devout women when they were all surprised to see that the sandals of the Infant Jesus were dirty with mud and sand and also looked a bit worn. Their astonishment grew as they saw that the hem and the lower part of the Holy Virgin's dress was wet and muddy and worn.

But the garment was new! And the Tabernacle was dry! How was it possible? They alerted the Prior of the convent. The garment was examined but no one could give an explanation, not even Brother Bernardo of Saint Catherine, the Commissioner of the Holy Office. All they could do was wait until God desired to make some revelation.

Later it was discovered that on 7 October 1613, the day dedicated to the Virgin of the Rosary, two galleys and five boats had been caught in a violent gale in the Philippines Sea. The people on board — Indios sentenced to forced labor and Spaniards — had barely managed to swim ashore. Among the Spaniards was an artilleryman, Francisco López, who was a truly evil man, a profligate, and a blasphemer. But he was also a devotee of Our Lady of the Rosary and every day he prayed to the Holy Virgin — even thieves have their favorite Saint, as the saying goes. The convicts managed to escape and then took to the mountains. The Spaniards went after them, but the Indios hurled stones down and injured or killed them.

Francisco López thought his last moment had come but he wanted to save his soul. He thus invoked Our Lady and begged her to let him confess to a priest. He fell to the ground, full of injuries and bleeding in every part of his body. He had even lost two fingers of one hand. On the damp ground his face and all his body swelled up. He was horribly disfigured. Worms started to devour him, wriggling into and out his wounds. The flesh started coming off his bones. For thirteen days Francisco had no food or drink; he was more dead than alive, but his only wish was to confess his sins.

Finally he saw a soldier named Gonzalo Salgado approaching, and he asked him to find him a confessor. Salgado wanted to take him to his boat but at the sight of the putrefying body the Indios threatened to run away to the mountains if he brought Francisco anywhere near the boat. So Salgado alerted his companions from the galley. Some of them came to where Francisco was but nobody could recognize him, not even his friends. They gave him something to eat and some wine but he refused everything, as he could neither eat nor drink. A doctor came too, but he could do nothing for Francisco — his body was covered in sores. Finally a Franciscan friar arrived and Francisco was able to confess. He died immediately afterwards, as only his desire to confess had kept him alive in his terrible condition. The men from the galley placed him in a boat, after tying his hands around a candle, one of those that the Dominicans bless to help people die in peace. Despite a strong wind that threatened the boat, the candle stayed alight for hours until it was taken out of his hands when his body was lowered into the grave. Only then did the candle flicker out, in the hands of the man who had taken it.

The miracle was ascertained in 1621. It was established to have taken place when the women had found the image of Our Lady of the Rosary with her dress wet and the sandals of the Infant Jesus dirty and worn, as if He had walked a great distance along a steep path. Our Lady had thus been wearing the dress when she went in aid of Francisco López. The dress was displayed in 1621 in the Dominican church and the local people came to worship and kiss it. The devotion to the Most Holy Virgin grew and many miracles happened both within and without the city.

The dress was kept in a small glass coffer. It was carried to the sick and to women in labor and placed over them. Every day there were new miracles. She caused milk to come to women who had none. In Manila, Maria Escudero was about to die and had confessed *in articulo mortis*. Her baby had twice shown its head and twice disappeared again inside. The Most Holy Virgin's dress was placed over the woman and all the people present invoked her aid with great devotion. Soon after, the baby was born and immediately baptized. The mother was safe too.

Many other women in labor were saved by Our Lady of the Rosary. Lady Catalina Dinguin, John Baptist Mejía's wife, was at death's door. The poor woman could not hear nor speak and she was dribbling from the mouth. Two Dominican friars arrived just in time carrying the Most Holy Virgin's dress. They placed it over the woman and intoned the hymn *Ave maris stella*. As soon as they reached the verse "Monstra te esse matrem", the woman gave birth to a child, after which she started talking again, a sign that she was well.

VIII.
Who Could Take His Place in the Philippines?

Brother Giordano immediately obtained his destination, as did all his companions. He was assigned to the mission in the Cagayan valley, on the northern tip of the island of Luzon, where the pygmy Negritos lived. These people covered themselves in tree bark. They built a light roofing over their heads and during the rainy season they lived in huts on stilts covered over by leaves. They got their food by hunting, fishing, and foraging.

The missionaries' work had not been easy in these parts either. The Filipinos worshiped what they called *anitos,* believing there was a good *anito,* which brought them all the good things that happened to them, and a bad *anito,* which caused all the bad things. They worshiped the good one so that it would grant them good things, and the bad one to placate it to make sure it did them no harm. The Filipinos would not undertake anything without seeking the *anitos'* protection. Before moving into a new home, they scrupulously followed a prescribed ritual. If a bird of ill omen entered their home, they would either demolish the house or make a thousand sacrifices in order to be able to live there again. The same happened when they bought something, before they put it in their home. Their houses were always full of objects and equipment required for sacrifices, which were sometimes strangely similar to the rituals of our own Holy Church. They even had their own kind of holy water and at Masi they used a special sort of water to wash their children in order to assure them of good fortune and a long life.

If after leaving home the Filipinos met another person who sneezed, they would hurry back, even if they were already a day's journey away. If the same thing happened while they were working, they would break off their toil. If they heard the call of a bird of ill omen they would stop whatever they were doing. Even if they were at war, they would stop fighting. The same happened if a bird flew to the left or if it pointed its beak at someone or in a certain direction.

Before sowing, they solemnly celebrated for three days. The men danced, ate, and drank until they fell to the ground and abandoned themselves to acts of dissolution. The women did the same, even if they did not drink. If they set out on a journey by sea or river, they would throw some of their food into the water in honor of the *anito*, so that it would be placated and their journey would be successful.

The Filipinos believed that when one of them died his soul had to cross a river or a lagoon in a boat owned by an ancient boatman. To pay this man for the crossing, they attached some money to the dead person's arm. They also believed that no woman could undertake the crossing unless her hands were colored black, according to their custom. They buried the dead with food for the journey and oil for their body, as well as clothes and some gold in case it should be needed. If the dead person was someone important, one or two slaves would be buried alive with him so that they could serve him. He would be buried in a pretty field full of flowers so that he could live a pleasant life, eating and drinking and resting until he returned once again to this world: for the Filipinos were convinced that their loved ones would return to live on earth one day. When one of the chiefs lost a son or a brother or a wife, everyone had to go into mourning and observe a long period of abstinence. They could not even eat rice, which in those lands was their bread, or drink wine, which they could scarcely go without, nor could meat or fish pass their lips. They were allowed to eat only roots and the fruits of the earth, and to drink water. This sometimes lasted for years, according to the importance of the dead person and their love for him. All the inhabitants of the village waited for the mourning to end. When they deemed that enough time had gone by and that their leader deserved to live a better life, they would buy a slave. They would all contribute to the cost and present the slave to their chief, who would cut the slave's throat in front of everyone. The mourning would then be over and they would all go to drink together.

These people were continuously at war, for all sorts of reasons. Sometimes the villages would reach an agreement, before actually starting a war, even when they were not at peace. This agreement could not however be reached without some bloodshed and the side that was at fault, or was weaker, had to buy a slave and hand him over to the other side. This poor devil would then be killed and everyone would strike him, even after he was dead. They would cut him up in pieces and everyone would be happy for a while. In their wars they spared neither women nor children nor the aged. The more people they killed, the more heroic they were considered to be, and they were rewarded with special decorations that no one else would dare to wear.

The Filipinos were vindictive, arrogant, envious, and prone to drunkenness and every other vice. Husbands easily left their wives, and wives their husbands, in order to remarry. They were all married in sin and this gave the missionaries a lot of work when they had to dispense the sacrament of marriage.

In the mountains and valleys there were huts with little statues and idols. The Filipinos would go there on pilgrimages to ask graces for their health and all their needs, great and small. In exchange, they would offer sacrifices, gold, precious stones, and the like. The sick would go to certain places of special devotion, according to their illness, in order to beg to be healed. There they would eat, and when they returned home they would leave behind them the pots and other objects they had used for the feast, because this was a sacrifice and everything used had to be offered to the *anito*.

They believed that the *anito* entered the body of the priestesses in order to give answers through them. The witch-priestesses demanded whatever was needed to placate the *anito* and to obtain its benevolence in order to obtain good health or some other desire. If they were paid, they promised to heal the sick and raise the dead. They killed certain types of birds and rubbed the blood on the bodies of the sick; and they used certain types of oil and other things while they recited their prayers.

The missionaries burned the idols and smashed the little boxes that contained the offerings. These were located in shaded places, hidden away among the ravines, the bamboo plantations, and the dense trees. No Filipino would violate them or touch the leaves of these trees, for they were sacred. The missionaries took the gold, the stones, and all the other offerings. They burned everything and threw the ashes into the sea or the rivers, as the astonished and fearful Indians watched. The missionaries also saved the lives of many children who would have been sacrificed to the idols or had their throats slit — the Indians used the blood to anoint the sick. The priestesses trembled with rage to see such destruction and also at the sight of their followers being taken away from them. They could see that their end was nigh, and they said they could see the *anitos* in the shape of buffaloes and black men wandering about the fields and complaining at being driven from their huts.

The Filipinos had not exactly taken a liking to the missionaries. To their eyes, the monks were little more than barbarians, with their white teeth, which was something the Filipinos could not abide — their own teeth they painted black. They applied to their teeth the juice of an aromatic leaf that they chewed all the time, the effect of which was to make them feel good from head to toe. They persecuted the missionaries in every way possible. They would not sell them water, wood, or food, hoping they would just go away. They also accused them of horrible doings. An Indian woman of distinguished origin was found to be pregnant without being married, and her relatives had therefore resolved to bury her alive, together with the man responsible, according to ancient law. So they tormented her to find out who the man was. The woman pronounced the name of Father Bernardo of Saint Catherine, the monks' Superior. Her family took her word and went to the Father, bent on revenge. The friar tried to calm them down and they returned to the woman to ask her when she had conceived. This was told and it was thus demonstrated that Father Bernardo had not been in the village at the time. But the same Father saved the woman from certain death.

When the Filipinos realized that the missionaries did not die after destroying their idols and their offerings, they ceased to fear the *anitos* and the priestesses and asked to be baptized. Many were converted and asked the missionaries to stay. The chief of one village even imprisoned a missionary — the man was afraid he might leave without baptizing his children. He begged the missionary to settle in his village, since everyone there wanted to become a Christian. In another village, some soldiers sent by a Spaniard to stop the construction of a church met a tragic end. The local people said, "They died because they were against the Church."

Many freed their slaves and released people from the bonds of usury; they returned things they had taken unlawfully or placed them at the missionaries' feet. It was a great consolation to see the men on one side and the women on the other praying together at dusk, around a Cross that usually stood in the village square.

Often the Spaniards did not behave like Christians in those far-off lands and this surprised the Filipinos. However, they were occasionally reminded of their duties. One brave man from Pata, the local governor, provided a passing Spaniard with rich hospitality in his own home and lavished all he could on him. But the traveler was not satisfied and said he wanted an Indian woman for the night. He was about to give the governor some jewels with which to buy him a woman but the governor refused to accept them and do what was asked of him, saying it was not right and that no one should do such a thing, especially as the man had just taken Holy Communion. Instead of acknowledging his mistake, the soldier of the Catholic King flew into a rage and threatened to beat the governor unless he did what he was told. At this the Filipino governor turned his back to the soldier, bowed his head, and said, "Hit me as much as you like, but I will not do what you ask me." The Spaniard beat him and the Filipino, a man of great physical strength who could have gobbled the bully up in one mouthful, suffered with great patience as he would not offend his God.

Once, an Indian woman, a slave in the same village, was struggling with a Spaniard who wanted to ravish her, even though he had taken Holy Communion only a few days earlier. She said, "But what are you doing? You take Communion and then you dare to commit such a sin?"

It was because of such arrogance that the Filipinos sometimes rebelled. That is what happened on 6 November 1621, in a remote part of New Segovia. On the previous Friday, the local people had erected a large and beautiful Cross in front of the church at Abuatan, amid expressions of great joy and devotion to the Lord. The following Sunday the church and some nearby houses were set on fire. A Dominican father, Alonso Hernández, who happened to be at Abuatan, tried to intervene and asked the local people their reasons for behaving in such a way. If the missionaries had treated them badly, they should take their revenge on him for the injustices they had suffered. The Filipinos replied that it was neither because of wrongs received from the missionaries nor out of hatred towards them, but because they were tired of the harassment they received from the Spaniards. The Filipinos advised Alonso to leave, as they could not guarantee his safety: some drunken Indian might cut his head off. The missionary had to go to Pilitan, the souls of which were entrusted to him.

At Pilitan it looked like a normal Sunday. But suddenly there was a great racket. It was the inhabitants of Abuatan who had come in great crowds, all naked and covered in oil, and armed to the teeth, intent on persuading the people to rise up with them against the Spaniards. One of the leaders, Cutapay, who had grown up in the Dominican church and as a younger man had been a sacristan and then a precentor, was now the Governor of Abuatan, and he rushed to the church to warn the Father of what was happening, urging him to flee before anyone harmed him. But as they were talking in the cloister, one of his brothers came along. He was another leader of the revolt and showed no consideration for the friar. But when Cutapay rebuked him, he calmed down and showed respect to the holy father.

Hundreds of Indians had arrived. The Father spoke to them, calling them his children. He tried to convince them that what they were doing was a mistake and warned them of the risk they were running. If they had been ill treated by the missionaries and that was the reason for their flight, then they should kill him: he should pay for the wrongs they had suffered. He told them not to abandon the faith he had preached for so many years and their hope of salvation. Otherwise they would pay in hell for their rebellion. Some of the Indians declared that they were not against the missionaries and that, on the contrary, they wanted and loved them. They told the Father they respected him and that they were rebelling only against Spanish oppression. He and the other missionaries were free to go to their villages, as long as they did not bring the Spaniards with them. The friar promised them the Spaniards would not hurt them or punish them for the rebellion. He would stay with them and they could take his life if any of them were injured. But the rebels paid no heed and some of them started burning the houses and shouting for war. Cutapay reprimanded them, for he did not want them to cause the Father any sorrow while he still remained. He thus ordered them to extinguish the fire and restore order. The friar returned to speak to them, but to no avail. The rebels asked him to leave and to take the silver and vestments from the vestries of the churches at Pilitan and Abuatan with him. They also gave him a boat and some rowers so that he could reach safer shores.

After he left, the rebels vented their hatred, burning houses, drinking, and threatening the lives of anyone who opposed their fury or refused to follow them. But a number of people secretly followed the missionaries, some leaving behind them their children, others their father and mother, and others their possessions. At Abuatan it was hell. The church was looted. The women wore the frontals as skirts, and put the tabernacle curtains and altar cloths on their heads. They even wore the priests' habits and showed disrespect for the image of the Most Holy Virgin of the Rosary, one of the most beautiful in the province and indeed in all the islands. Someone had the nerve to stab it in the nose, saying, "Let's see if she bleeds." But an Indian managed to save the statue and took it with him to a Christian village, where everyone welcomed it and cried to see that the Most Holy Virgin had been so badly treated. The new year, 1622, at last brought peace. Father Pedro de Santo Tomás, who had been the vicar of these churches, managed to placate the rebels and make them repent for what they had done.

There were martyrs too among the island missionaries. On Sunday 8 June 1625 another band of Indians from the New Segovia province rebelled, those of Nuestra Señora del Rosario de Fotol and San Lorenzo de Capitanan. They turned their backs on the missionaries and took to the mountains, as they had tried to do before. They went to Father Alonso García and found him at table with a lay brother, Onofre Palao. The Indians butchered them with hideous violence, chopped the Father's body into pieces, and fed it to the pigs. They set the churches on fire, cut the face of a figure of Christ, and broke the body in two. But soon they saw the error of their ways and wanted the missionaries and the churches back.

These were the people Brother Giordano of Santo Stefano found himself among. He did his utmost to understand them and to accomplish his mission. He soon learned the local dialect and he was thus able to preach, to make himself understood, and to take confession. And some extraordinary events occurred there. One day, when Brother Giordano noticed a soldier he had never noticed before, he went up to him and asked him, "Why don't you think of yourself and of your soul? It is many years since your last proper confession."

The soldier was amazed, for the Dominican Father was right. He told another priest what had happened, who in turn told someone else.

Another day, as he was celebrating Holy Mass, Brother Giordano suddenly stopped. A Spaniard who was listening to Mass was surprised and started observing the Father with great attention, to see if he needed anything. He noticed that the priest had an expression of great happiness on his face and that he was looking up in the air as if he could see or hear someone talking to him. Brother Giordano then called the Spaniard over and told him what he had heard: that he should not continue to say Mass because the wine he had been given was mixed with seawater. The Spaniard tasted the wine and realized that it was exactly as the Father had said.

One day, at Malagueg, Father Luis Gandullo heard a kindly voice as he was preparing the Chalice to celebrate Holy Mass. The voice said, "Look at this wine." As he had tried the wine the day before, he did not try it again, fearing he was being led into temptation. So he started Mass and as he was getting to the Consecration he heard the same voice again, only this time speaking more hurriedly. He went on but as soon as he drank the wine he realized it had turned into vinegar.

Brother Giordano often did penance. He mortified his body with sackcloth and lashed himself with a chain. Unflaggingly he wanted to devote all his energy to the needy, convert the Filipinos, and never spend a moment idle. His life belonged to God — it had to be wholly in the service of his God and of his fellow man. That was the reason he was there, in those remote lands inhabited by such savage and bloodthirsty people.

On 24 April 1627 the Provincial Chapter assigned the Friar from Santo Stefano to the Hospital House of Saint Gabriel at Binondo. This was a difficult mission among Manila's Chinese population. Brother Hyacinth was again to be his companion.

Thus Brother Giordano also dedicated himself to the sick with infinite patience and charity. He was a pauper among paupers, a true man of God. He bustled his way around the hospital rooms. He assisted the dying and baptized them. He had a word of comfort for all. He fed the sick with his own hands, washed them, and prayed with them. He neglected his own comfort and ate very little. His habit was rough and torn and his shoes were broken. He slept on wooden boards without a mattress or on the floor. And how many times he crossed the Pasig River! He even brought God's word to the Chinese in Parian, where many were the baptisms he performed.

And yet, even for such a humble, intelligent, and kindly friar, it was no easy task to be a missionary among the Chinese. They were brutish and, despite all his good works, he sometimes he had to suffer their insolence. Above all, Brother Giordano wanted to understand the Chinese. So he studied their language and learned it extraordinarily well, never however neglecting his duties in the hospital. While at a sick person's bedside or when others were asleep, or when chewing a morsel of food, he would write the treatise he had started on the religious sects of China, describing their origins and refuting their beliefs. However, he was never able to finish it because of all the work he had to do. He was always punctual for prayers. The Provincial Father Friar Miguel Ruiz described him as a perfect minister of the Gospel.

During the night of 13 March 1628, while Brother Giordano was performing his mission among the Chinese, a house in Parian caught fire. The flames quickly spread to the adjoining houses, which were made of bamboo and palm-trees. In a few hours all the houses were destroyed, except for a few that were sheltered by a grove of green trees and one or two others standing some way off. The fire even threatened to spread from another tall house to the church itself and the house of the Dominicans. Missionaries of other orders immediately came running up and with everyone's help they tried to stop the fire, throwing buckets of water on the Dominicans' wooden building, which was beginning to catch fire. A crowd of infidels stood there enjoying the scene, shouting, "Let's see if the God of the Christians will save their church." The Dominicans took the image of Our Lady of the Rosary from the church and held it up to the wind and to the fire, which was getting ever closer. Suddenly the wind changed direction and took the fire with it, and the church was saved. All those present, including the infidels, were astonished and shouted that a miracle had taken place, thanking the Most Holy Virgin and singing her praises.

In May 1629 Father Francisco de Herrera, Commissioner of the Holy Inquisition in the Philippine Islands and Prior of the Convent in Manila, was elected Provincial. The Provincial Chapter of 10 May 1631 recognized Brother Giordano's exceptional skills and assigned him to the Convent of Saint Dominic in Manila, with the title of Examiner of Confessors, *ratione idiomatis Sinarum*. Other friars were assigned to the same convent: Brother Hyacinth, who was still studying Japanese; Father Diego Aduarte, who was the Prior and gathered all the documents regarding the missions, observed everything that happened, and wrote about the lives and martyrdom of the Dominican saints; and Father Francisco de Paula, who had also studied in the convent of Saint Stephen in Salamanca and wrote of the lives of the brave missionaries in Japan.

Brother Giordano was undoubtedly in his element in this convent, a man of letters among other men of letters with whom he had so much common. But what he wanted most of all was to be allowed to go to Japan, where there was sore need of missionaries. He wanted to lay down his life for Christ there, and he never forgot that this was the reason why he had set off in the first place. All sorts of things in the convent in Manila reminded him of the sacrifice of the many who had suffered martyrdom in Japan. Among these objects was a damask-colored flag with the Name of Christ printed on it. It had probably belonged to a confraternity of that name, and the Dominican Fathers had taken it to Nagasaki when they went with other friars to their martyrs' death in September 1622.

The Friar from Santo Stefano was thus ready for this step but he dared not ask his superiors for the permission he so wanted — he suffered qualms of conscience. Other times he would request it with great humility, and again he would have doubts and think that he was being too insistent, that he was asking for something that was too big for him, and that he wanted to do something that only the Holy Martyrs had ever done. As always, he put himself in God's hands and humbly awaited his superiors' decisions. The friars knew how resolutely Brother Giordano desired to go to Japan, and they considered his resigned humility and his behavior to be even more worthy in the eyes of God than his decision to leave Sicily and Spain, when he had forsaken his country and his family in order to follow his inspiration and his chosen path. His resignation now allowed him to prevail upon himself, precisely in that which he most desired: only the power of God's grace could subdue him, for he was passionate by nature and fiery in his desires.

But Brother Giordano's superiors could see the fruits of his presence in Manila. There was great need for him there and it would not have been easy to replace him. Who else had his culture? Who knew Chinese and the Cagayan dialect so perfectly? Who understood the Filipinos' mentality and customs so well? And the task of evangelization was not yet complete. Thus they tried to dissuade him from his intent and attempted to quench his thirst for being a real missionary by assigning him once again to the Hospital of Saint Gabriel at Binondo.

With his customary modesty, Brother Giordano reiterated his request to be allowed to go to Japan. And at last, in 1632, with his superiors' blessing, his wish was granted, when a new missionary expedition to those lands was being prepared, just as the shogun Yemitsu was venting all his hatred on the Christians.

IX.
Japan, Land of Martyrs

The missionaries knew what they were about to experience and had often spoken of it. When Saint Francis Xavier had arrived in Japan in 1549, the Japanese had not been able to resist his words and soon began to be converted, aristocrats too, even a son of the Emperor Goyozu and the Governor of Nagasaki, Terazawa Hirotaka. Several *daimyos* and many ordinary citizens, as well as large numbers of poor peasants, had followed their example: it has always been so. The first impression the Christians had formed of the Japanese was thus that of hospitable, kind, and inquisitive folk who were eager to learn and know the truth.

But soon suspicion spread among the Japanese. Persecutions started and continued with greater ferocity than ever. Even the Christians became intolerant of other religions: they were pleased when they saw the shoguns persecuting Buddhism and they too persecuted it; the Jesuits, who had obtained from the *daimyo* of Omura the concession to administer Nagasaki and the right to collect the harbor taxes, had publicly condemned the bonzes' rituals and traditions and set fire to a Buddhist temple in the town to make way for a Christian church. But the bonzes had taken their revenge, persuading the shogun that the Christians were a serious menace and that they should be condemned and expelled for the good of Japan and the Japanese. And so it was that in 1587 the shogun Toyotomi Hideyoshi pronounced an edict expelling all foreign missionaries in Japan:

Having been informed by our faithful counselors that foreign missionaries have reached our States and preach a law contrary to that of Japan and that they have had the audacity to destroy temples dedicated to Kami and Hotoke, and even though this offence alone deserves extreme punishment, we wish nevertheless to demonstrate our compassion and accordingly command that on pain of death they shall leave Japan within twenty days. At the end of such period, we further order that if any of them are discovered in our States they shall be arrested and punished like our worst criminals. As for the

Portuguese merchants, we allow them to enter our ports in order to carry on their customary business and to stay in our States, provided that our commerce draws benefit from theirs. But we forbid them to bring any foreign missionary into our country, on pain of confiscation of their boats and their goods.

But Hideyoshi was one who easily changed his mind and behaved as if he had forgotten the edict; for in 1593 four Franciscans arrived and not only had the shogun permitted them to stay in Japan but he even agreed to let them build their churches. Once again he began to have doubts, or someone caused him to have doubts about the missionaries: who was behind them? Could Spain be sending them on ahead to conquer Japan? So he remembered the edict of 1587 and condemned twenty-six Christians, six Franciscans, three Jesuits, and seventeen laymen: they were crucified in 1597 and Pope Urban VIII beatified them in 1627.

The Japanese lords could not be content that Christians should obey their own spiritual fathers rather than the temporal authorities, worship rebels condemned to death, and glorify themselves for dying on the cross like Jesus Christ. They were convinced that the Christians were a sect of fanatics, perverse and dangerous for the Empire, determined to spread their form of law, which — the Japanese said — would eventually destroy the legitimate law of divine Japan. They would not bow down to the barbarians from the South. And other edicts were pronounced against the Christians.

In 1602 the first Augustines and Dominicans too had reached Japan: they arrived from the Philippines and they had been invited by the *daimyo* of Satsuma, a fief of the island of Kyushu. They landed at the islet of Koshiki, opposite Satsuma, and then proceeded to continental Japan, where they built the Church of Our Lady of the Rosary.

The Japanese were especially curious to see these Dominican friars, whose virtues were known far and wide; they carefully studied everything about them, their black and white habits (colors of which they too approved), their gestures and their words, their culture and their singular humility, their sense of mercy, their refusal of all comforts and their incredible sacrifices, their merriness and their poverty. They were much attracted by these virtues, as also by their good manners and by the fact that they all behaved in the same way.

The Jesuits protested — in their opinion they should be the ones to evangelize Japan, and they cited the Breve they had obtained from Pope Gregory XIII: Japan was to be the exclusive field of mission of the Company of Jesus. And therefore missionaries of other orders should leave. But the Franciscans, the Dominicans, and the Augustines replied that His Holiness was ill-informed and that he could not prevent the seed they too spread in Japan from growing; they wanted to play their part and requested the creation of a number of bishoprics in those lands: there was much to be done, there was work for everyone.

They even resorted to accusations. The Mendicants accused the Jesuits of neglecting the poor and of trading in silver and silk and alleged that the Bishop of Japan, a Jesuit, was never to be found in his official seat. The Jesuits denied all this and accused the friars of not respecting the canonical laws and of annulling valid marriages; they also blamed them for the deterioration of relationships between the Japanese and the Christians, and consequently for the persecutions that were exterminating them all. They sought some sort of compromise and for this reason accepted many elements of the native cults and customs — they had even expressed the words God and Heaven in Buddhist terms. The Dominicans and the Franciscans were horrified; they could not brook such methods.

Pope Paul V listened to the pleas of the Mendicant Orders, and his Breve of 11 June 1608 authorized all men of religion to go to Japan to preach the word of God. But this was not enough; the Jesuits did not give up and there was an outcry: the suspicion arose that certain missionaries might care less about the salvation of souls and more about privilege and power. The Superiors of the Mendicants administered the Sacrament of Confirmation; the Jesuits protested, maintaining that only the Bishop could do this.

That the Dominicans had converted several Japanese — including the samurai Shikityemon, who had died a martyr in 1608 — could not be denied. Within a few years their missions had become so numerous that the lords had begun to be alarmed: they increasingly feared that these missionaries were in fact spies sent by the King of Spain to conquer their land, as the Dutch maintained. Even the daimyo of Satsuma had changed his mind and expelled the Dominicans from his fief, and other daimyos had done the same. And so the missionaries had gathered near Nagasaki and Omura.

Everyone remembered the martyrdom that many Christians suffered in 1613; a notorious forger of coins was also crucified, a Christian, one of those who caused such damage and were such an obstacle to the work of the missionaries. Some were left to burn to death over a slow fire. In January 1614 another edict was pronounced for the total persecution of all Christians: the missionaries were to be exterminated. However, some succeeded in remaining in Japan, including some Dominicans who went into hiding but were unable to do anything to prevent the infidels' work of destruction: churches, houses, and cemeteries were pulled down and all symbols of Christianity were effaced. And soon the missionaries in hiding began to be caught and punished.

The persecution continued uninterruptedly for years and thousands of Christians were martyred. But the Holy Faith had already begun to put down its roots. A special devotion to Our Lady of the Rosary had spread in Japan and many people expressed the desire to have an image of her, and in the end the Dominican friars had had copies printed for the faithful to take home. They derived great comfort from reciting the Holy Rosary in front of her. Nagasaki had become the metropolis of Christianity in Japan and infidels arrived from every corner to listen to the missionaries' words and to be baptized. And the more people became Christians, the higher the number of martyrs.

Many inhabitants of the city were condemned in 1622; everyone remembered the tenth of September, the day of the Great Martyrdom, when during the execution the vast multitude of spectators broke into song and prayers and psalms in praise of God. In recent years there was no counting the number of Martyrs, even children: either burned alive over a slow fire; or cooked slowly in a mixture of boiling water, sulphur, resin, and oil; or kept in freezing water; or crucified; or beheaded; or gradually cut to pieces with saws made of canes; or buried alive to the waist and cut with a sharp katana, as in October 1630, when a man was severed from the left shoulder to the right arm with a blade so thin that when with his left hand he made the sign of the cross over his forehead and down to his mouth, his body split in two.

Others were condemned to death by starvation — the doors of their houses were boarded up and fathers and mothers felt their hearts break at the sight of their children begging in tears for food, their cries gradually growing feebler. These cruel tormentors tortured children in the presence of their parents, and wives in the presence of their husbands, declaring that they would leave them alone if they did but renounce their faith. Others were crowded together in enclosures out in the open in the cold and rain until they died. And there were some that the Japanese wanted to keep alive but mutilated, with fingers missing or even with no fingers and toes at all, or without a nose, or with a sign of the cross branded on their forehead with a red-hot iron, to serve as an example and to discourage Christians or whoever wished to follow them, wherever they went.

The Japanese could not understand how these men could bear such suffering rather than renounce their religion; they would not have it and they studied new sorts of torture, ever more efficient. Cutting off heads or roasting people over a slow fire appeared to many to be too humane a punishment, good only for common criminals; for these Christians something special had to be thought of, something that would terrorize them to such an extent that they would no longer persevere in their intent. And so it was that they invented the combined torture of the gallows and the pit. Sometimes they would have the prisoners tended by doctors so that they could torment them further and dismay them with the repetition of the torture. But the effect on the Christians who witnessed these martyrdoms or even only heard of them was often the opposite of what the Japanese had hoped for: they saw that the example of the condemned prisoners made people even surer of their faith, and this increased the torturers' rage.

It was forbidden to give the missionaries hospitality, on pain of death for those who disobeyed; they would be burned alive with their entire family. And anyone who in any way was on familiar terms with the missionaries was arrested, as also anyone found with a Christian book in his hands. There was a reward for anyone who helped catch a missionary, and in the public squares it was possible to see silver coins with the following announcement: "This silver shall be given to whomsoever shall find a thief or a missionary"; the friars remembered that Jesus Christ was crucified between two thieves.

But the missionaries prepared themselves for all that might befall them; they even had specific guides to help them face torture and the final torment, such as *Exhortations to Martyrdom*, which the missionaries in Japan compiled after the edict of 1614. This work prescribed how the persecuted were to behave: they were not to not hate their torturers, but to pray to God that they might repent; while they were being tortured they were to have Christ's Passion before their eyes, sure in the belief that the Virgin Mary and the Angels and Saints could see their battle from heaven, that the Angels awaited their souls, crown in hand, and that God would give them special help; and they were to proclaim their faith in full view of the spectators in order to induce them to seek their salvation, saying for example that there was no other means but the religion of Christ that could save them and that there was no greater joy than to sacrifice one's life in order to testify to the truth of that religion, which was the only way to eternal happiness. God Himself would inspire them with what to say and what to do.

X.
He Looked a Real Chinaman

All these Dominicans wanted to go to Japan simply because there was such a need for missionaries. But how were they to get there? The only people who could take them to the islands were Chinese merchants and everyone knew that if paid enough they never said no, but they were untrustworthy characters: sometimes, after taking the agreed sum, during the journey they would kill the missionaries they were carrying, and often they would denounce them as soon as they reached land in order to obtain other rewards.

There was another problem too: one needed the permission of the Governor of the Philippines and he would have nothing of it, for he had absolute orders from his faraway king to prevent missionaries from leaving for Japan, in view of the way many of them had ended up — it was like sending them to slaughter and the good king was bound to take the lives of his subjects to heart. And those who did succeed in reaching Japan found it no easy task to elude the surveillance of the guards, who had strict orders not to admit missionaries for whatever reason.

But the Governor was ill, a circumstance that was turned to advantage: all the Orders were quick to action, with three Jesuits preparing to leave, two Franciscans, two Augustines, two Recollects, and two Dominicans — Brother Giordano from Santo Stefano and Brother James from Santa Maria. They were not to leave all together, lest they might arouse suspicion, so they split up into different boats and left Manila on different days.

The Dominicans' superiors had to pay one hundred and fifty Japanese reals for the boat, a very high price, but the Chinese took everything into account, including the risk they were running in transporting missionaries while the worst ever persecution against them was taking place in Japan.

On the ninth of July 1632 Brother Giordano was able to leave. He looked a real Chinaman, as the merchants desired, so that he should not be discovered: he spoke Chinese and he was dressed Chinese-style, just like them. His traveling companions were Father Sebastian Vieyra, a Portuguese Jesuit who held the position of Vice-Provincial and Administrator of the Bishopric of Japan, and the two Spanish Franciscans.

There were many perils and hardships during the voyage and the boat almost capsized and sank in the stormy sea. Close by the island of Tabaco a violent wind forced them to interrupt the voyage. It was then that all the passengers and sailors realized who they were traveling with missionaries. They protested and the sailors wanted to take them back to Manila. The travelers included eleven Japanese Christians, some of whom had however denied their religion, and one of them, a sour old fellow with one foot in the grave, began to pick on Brother Giordano and the Franciscans; with merciless irony he admonished them for being mad enough to want to be missionaries in Japan: first, because they knew neither the language nor the customs of the Japanese yet had the presumptuousness to claim the gift of tongues like the Apostles and Saint Francis Xavier; second, because they were going to Japan against the orders of the Pope and the King of Spain, thus violating their duties both as Christians and as Spaniards; and third, because if they really wanted martyrdom they could go elsewhere to look for it and spare many Christians in Japan the risk of falling into apostasy.

As soon as it was possible, they resumed their navigation as best they could. But a terrible hurricane began to rage, lasting three full days; again it looked as if they would sink at any moment and they all confessed. The storm blew over. Now the Chinese wanted to make for the coast of China, but the Japanese were against this and the boat headed north. Brother Giordano and the other three missionaries were locked together in a cabin and told not to breathe a word; they also had to fast.

Eventually, on the last day of July, land was sighted and three days later the boat entered a port in the islands of Goto, west of Nagasaki. The missionaries' fear of discovery grew and they were still kept locked up in their cabin — they nearly fainted for lack of air. They decided to disembark and they asked a trader from Shimabara to take them to the coast of the Nagasaki peninsula, agreeing on a price of two hundred and fifty taes. They docked on the twelfth of August and split up, each on his separate way.

Things went no better for Brother James of Santa Maria, who traveled with two Jesuits and some Japanese traders. He was dressed like them and carried katanas, and he had the advantage of being able to speak Japanese, being Japanese himself. Instead of twenty days, the usual duration of this voyage, they were at sea for five months because of the storms; food and water were in short supply and they were nearly wrecked; the boat was driven by the winds as far as the coast of Korea. When towards the end of 1632 they landed at Satsuma, south of the island of Kyushu, Brother James had not one single black hair on his head — he was only fifty years of age and when he set off his hair was jet-black.

And then it happened that the sailors and the Chinese and Japanese merchants who had ferried them across quarreled over the shares of money for the hiring of the boat, and one of them took his revenge on the owner of the vessel by going to the authorities to report the missionaries' voyage and their arrival. The result was that he was immediately sentenced to death along with his accomplices. While awaiting execution, they remembered what Brother Giordano had said during the journey and they asked if they could be baptized so that they could die to die as Christian souls, but there was no one to satisfy their request.

XI.
Like a Dove that Knows not Where to Come to Land

As soon as he landed, Brother Giordano went straight to the town of Nagasaki to seek out Brother Dominic, the Vicar of the Mission, and to put himself at his disposal. When he arrived, at around nine o'clock at night, he was exhausted. He turned into a street just as the caretaker was closing the door. Brother Giordano thought it was the door to the Vicar's house and that the Vicar was opening the door to greet him. So he threw himself into the caretaker's arms and greeted him in Spanish. The caretaker, a Japanese, was much alarmed and Brother Giordano almost spent his first night in jail. However, Brother Dominic, who lived in the same street, heard the din and came out with all the other people who lived there in the house. He put the caretaker's mind at rest, and Brother Giordano was allowed in to spend the night in the house. As soon as day came, he was sent two hundred leagues away.

As always, the Brother from Santo Stefano felt that his first duty was to learn the language of the country of his mission. Very soon he was able to speak and understand Japanese, which boggled the mind of most people who tried to learn it; but he had a flair for languages — God was on his side and granted to him the same gift he had granted to the Apostles.

Brother Giordano wasted no time and immediately started to devote himself to the work for which he had gone to Nagasaki. However, things seemed to start off in the worst of ways. As soon as they landed, the first thing the Chinese merchants did, as usual, was to raise accusations against the missionaries they had brought from Manila. The shogun was enraged. He removed the governor of Nagasaki, Uneme, and appointed two new governors, Soga Matazayemon and Imamura Denshiro, whose duty it was to annihilate the Christians. Anyone finding a missionary was promised one thousand silver taes and a free pardon for any crime he might have committed.

The first to be caught were the Recollect Fathers, and then Brother Luca of the Holy Spirit. Brother Giordano was almost captured with him, but Brother Dominic was caught. To find Brother Dominic his persecutors made a drawing of him, based on information about his person and personal aspect that they had obtained from people who knew him. They gave the sketch to numerous people who carried it about with them, hoping they might meet the friar and claim the promised reward. But in the end they managed to find him only because someone who knew Brother Dominic's whereabouts was tortured until he revealed where the friar was.

Many Christians were terrified and several renounced their faith. Even a mere sigh or an invocation was enough to give them away. If anyone heard them say, "Jesus and Mary!" they would immediately be reported to the judge and the reward would be claimed. Many abandoned their homes and all their belongings to escape to the mountains. They hid in caves, in water tanks, or in haystacks, like Brother Dominic, the friar from Biscay. But the soldiers rooted them out everywhere — they searched among the rocks, which they would roll this way and that, and set fire to the mountains where they thought the Christians might be hiding.

Brother Giordano had heard about all this before setting off for Japan. Brother Thomas of Saint Hyacinth had written a letter to the Provincial Superior in Manila informing him that all the Christians in Nagasaki had apostatized; that numerous traitors no better than Judas were zealously looking for the missionaries in order to claim the promised rewards; that all those who entered or left Nagasaki were asked whether they were Christians and to which sect they belonged (those who said they were Christians were forced to apostatize, even if they were foreigners, while those who refused to apostatize were martyred); that no missionary could enter the city or stay there a day, it was impossible to go to confession, and many died without the Sacraments.

The most dreaded sentence was the one the Japanese had most recently invented, the protracted *ana-tsurushi* torture, which involved use of a pit and the gallows. The victims were strung up for days and days, depending on their powers of resistance, dangling by the feet from the gallows, with their head free, stuck into a pit full of filth. Their sides would be held fast by wooden planks that closed off the pit.

To avoid capture, the missionaries could not spend two days in the same house or even in the same street. They had to move every night, even when it was freezing and they had no shoes, in snow, rain, or mud. When the weather was bad, they thanked God's grace, as they could move around without being seen. They could go into people's homes and spread God's word, which was their sole reason for being in Japan. But they had to shun the sun and the moon. At night they could administer the Sacraments and help those in need. They dressed as peasants, as merchants with cloak and sword, even as samurai and Japanese beggars with straw sandals on their feet. But people were frightened to let them into their homes. Even if they were willing to open their door, the neighbors would not allow it for if a missionary was caught, not only those with him in the house would be killed but also all the neighbors in the next five houses. And servants could not be trusted either.

But when Brother Dominic, the Vicar Father, was caught in July 1633, Brother Giordano decided to descend from the mountains to Nagasaki to get fresh news. Recalling the misadventures he had suffered since leaving Luzon, he wrote as follows:

One letter can scarce describe all the hardships and adversities that befell me in the boat after I departed from the island of Luzon. Twice our lives were imperilled, once in a terrible storm that tossed us within a stone's throw of an island. Only a miracle saved us. And after we reached Japan, there were even more storms and dangers.

When the Recollect Fathers were taken prisoner, soon after we arrived, I was almost taken too. I was also nearly captured when they were searching for Father Luca of the Holy Spirit and myself. The man we most trusted came looking for us together with the followers of the persecutors, and if I escaped it was thanks to God. Now I have heard of the arrest of the Vicar Father, Brother Dominic de Erquicia, and I have come down from the mountains in order to learn more.

The letter went on to describe the difficulties of hiding in the mountains by day and of working by night, *like a dove that knows not where to come to land.*

On the thirteenth of August, Brother Dominic was martyred in Nagasaki. He was hanged by the feet with his head and half his body down a well. He died the following day. His body was burned and the ashes thrown in the sea. His Japanese attendant Francis Shoyemon likewise suffered martyrdom. His body was dismembered with a curved katana sword and thrown on a fire. Fourteen other Christians suffered martyrdom with them, including three women and a child.

On the day commemorating the Assumption of the Virgin Mary, the same day that he was ordained, the Japanese Dominican friar James of Santa Maria faced martyrdom by the gallows and the pit. He died, after two days of agony, on the seventeenth of August, the same day that he took his vows. His ashes too were thrown in the sea. His Japanese catechist Michael Kurobioye suffered the same torture a few days later. He it was who, unable to bear the pain, had revealed Brother James's whereabouts to his torturers. But he never renounced his faith.

On the eighteenth of October, St Luke's Day, Father Luca, four Jesuits, Brother Matthew, Brother Dominic, and others were condemned to *ana-tsurushi* in Nagasaki. The Jesuit and Vice-Provincial of the Society Father Christopher Ferreira was able to hold out for only five hours, after which he renounced his faith and began to co-operate with his persecutors. The Japanese rejoiced and even suspended the torture of Father Luca and some others. They took the missionaries back to jail, hoping they would follow the Jesuit's example, and made them many promises. However, Father Luca kept on repeating the same answer, that the Japanese were wasting their time and were toiling to no avail. He said he only yearned for his God and was happy to die for Him. And he asked to be taken back to his companions.

Word of the Jesuit's renunciation soon spread and caused great scandal. The Fathers of the Society sought to persuade him to repent but did not succeed. Many commented, "And the Jesuits were supposed to be the only ones who could evangelize Japan!" However, there were also Jesuits who suffered martyrdom bravely, including Father Giovanni Matteo Adami, a Sicilian from Mazara. Some people wanted to be sure that Brother Luca had not renounced, and accordingly went to the jail where he was locked up and called to him from the street. He reassured them from a window that his only wish was to die for the Holy Faith.

That had always been his fervent wish. On his way to jail after he was caught, he sang a *Te Deum*. Similar chants could be heard from inside the jail. The Franciscans imprisoned there sang the *Magnificat*, and the chorus was joined by the Dominicans outside. Brother Luca and a Jesuit who shared his cell even washed and kissed each other's feet in turn. This bewildered the guards, who asked them the meaning of their deeds, to which the missionaries replied that they were doing as Jesus had done with His disciples and that He had ordered them to do the same.

Night over, Brother Luca and the others were taken back to the torture chamber. The torturers were even more angered. They did not even want to wait for the Father to die after a long agony, setting an example for others, and they finished him off by hitting him with sticks and daggers while he was still hanging up. Then they cut him to pieces and burned him to ashes.

His Japanese assistants, Brother Matthew of the Rosary and the lay Brother Dominic Kakusuke, also suffered martyrdom. The good Dominic could have saved his life but chose to stay with Father Luca. He preferred to died for Christ rather than continue to live in a world of misery. And while he was being taken to jail, a young Christian man started shouting that he was his brother and also a servant of Father Luca — he too was taken to jail with the others: one martyr called another.

Thus only two Dominican missionaries were left in Japan: Brother Giordano, who became Vicar of the Mission, and Brother Thomas of Saint Hyacinth, a Japanese born on the island of Hirado, where the sermons of Saint Francis Xavier were still remembered. His parents had also been Christians, for which reason they had been sent to exile and later sentenced to death. After becoming an orphan, he was sent to the Jesuit College in Nagasaki and later had gone to Manila, where he became a Dominican. Some friars were perplexed that the Japanese should be allowed into the Order. These friars doubted that the Japanese, who by nature were so full of themselves, so arrogant and scornful of others, could ever become humble missionaries. But Brother Thomas won them over with his amiable behavior. Entering the order, he had taken the name of Hyacinth, after Saint Hyacinth, the holy saint of Poland, who was so dear to the Dominican friars. Brother Giordano had held him at the Baptismal Font.

There was another Dominican friar by the same name who had never succeeded in setting foot in Japan, however much he always wanted to. That was his reason for leaving Spain. This was Brother Hyacinth of the Rosary, Brother Giordano's favorite companion. He had prepared for the mission by studiously learning Japanese. But he had been killed in August 1633, as he was sailing to Japan, by the very Chinese who were taking him there. A Franciscan friar was also assassinated, and both missionaries had their ears and noses cut off and put in salt. When they arrived in Nagasaki, the Chinese took the ears and noses to the judges of the city and claimed their reward. The Chinese traitor did not however enjoy his reward for long, for he gambled it all away and died soon after from a haemorrhage. Despite being infidels, even his associates thought death was an appropriate punishment, sent from above because of his treachery. The only thing left of Brother Hyacinth was the Japanese-Spanish dictionary, a true relic, that he had published in Manila a few years before.

Brother Giordano continued to preach God's word, despite all he had heard and seen and even though threatened by capture. He was alone yet fearless, his thin face tight-drawn over his cheekbones. He roved around Nagasaki, the region of Omura, and the island of Kyushu, some twenty kilometers from Nagasaki. He continued to baptize, to confess, and to give encouragement to those who were beginning to waver after losing their spiritual father: some had not had Christian confession for over twenty years.

At Omura, he was given hospitality by Sister Marina, a young Tertiary Dominican. She had been born there and her virtue set an example to all Christians in the region. She wholeheartedly welcomed missionaries to her home and served them with devotion. She had given hospitality to the Dominican Father Louis Beltrán of Barcelona before he was martyred. He it was who had taken her into the Dominican Family and given her the habit of a Blessed sister. She had always been most faithful to her vows of obedience and chastity and lived in her home, like Saint Catherine of Siena. Brother Giordano needed her help in order to gain access to people's homes in Omura and to him she seemed a saint, the most valorous and saintly woman that Japan had ever seen. He even wrote her biography, which was later confiscated: for until the end of his days Brother Giordano strove to follow his other vocation, writing, always in the service and glory of the Lord.

While at Omura, the Friar from Santo Stefano fell so seriously ill that he feared he would die of his malady. But that was not the way he wanted to die. He therefore returned to Nagasaki for treatment and there he put himself in the hands of the Most Holy Virgin, begging her to heal him and let him live until he was killed in Christ's name. And in four or five days he was better. During those days Brother Thomas was of great comfort to him, and when Brother Giordano was out of danger Brother Thomas announced that he wanted to return to Omura to continue the mission and take over from Brother Giordano. But the convalescent missionary held him back, saying: "Brother, no one is to leave this place before the celebrations for the festivity of our Father!"

XII.
How Could He Bow to One Who Had no Respect for God?

Brother Giordano never stopped thanking the Most Holy Virgin and the Lord for his miraculous recovery: after only five days he was as before, he felt full of energy and above all eager to resume his mission in that land which had been consecrated by the martyrdom of so many Christians and where it must have seemed that the persecutors had long lost their wits.

The festivity for Saint Dominic the Patriarch was approaching and this had to be celebrated as tradition prescribed; Brother Giordano, with the help of Brother Thomas, wished to prepare for the event all the Christians he could find, by hearing their confession.

But in the very same period guards had been unleashed throughout Nagasaki to scour the most outlying areas: their orders were to arrest Brother Michael of Saint Joseph, an Augustine monk. They came close to where the two Dominicans were located, and the missionaries were forced to leave the town in order to safeguard the good man who was offering them hospitality, the other people in his house, and his neighbors: all Japanese were obliged to report the presence of missionaries — if they did not, they would receive the same treatment. And the number of Judases had increased still more, for the shogun Yemitsu, in a new edict against Christians pronounced on 28th February 1633, had promised one hundred silver coins to anyone reporting a missionary.

The friars found shelter in a hut at Misuyura, abandoned by the Japanese, a short distance from Nagasaki, where they found themselves on 4th August 1634, Saint Dominic's Day, praying and waiting until they could return to the city. But the hound-dogs got there too, and great was their rejoicing to find two pigeons rather than one in that abandoned nest; they arrested the missionaries and took them straight to Nagasaki, dragging them with a rope round their neck along the main streets, hands tied behind their back. They were followed by a vast throng of exultant soldiers and inquisitive onlookers — the din was incredible. The Christians too saw them passing by and they could not hold back their tears: they were losing their last great fathers and were even more alone than before.

They arrived in court and were presented to the judges, who were astonished to see Brother Giordano making not the slightest of bows to them, but standing erect, looking them in the eye with great dignity and determination, as if he were the judge: everyone in Japan, in the presence of such judges, lay prostrate with his hands and forehead on the ground. Brother Giordano disenchanted them by saying that men with such little respect and reverence for God in heaven and His holy law, men who ignored such undeniable obligations, did not deserve to be shown any form of courtesy, nor could they who violated the divine law of God expect the human laws of their kingdom to be observed.

The judges then addressed Brother Thomas and asked him if he was a missionary or a Christian; he too was resolute, emulating Giordano, his superior and his companion, replying like the martyr Saint Cyprian, just saying yes and only no when they asked him if he wished to apostatize.

They resumed the interrogation of the Friar from Santo Stefano and asked him who had brought him to Japan. Brother Giordano explained that he was a missionary of Saint Dominic and that the Lord had brought him to Japan to spread the truth, and that he had no fixed abode on earth; that he was always wandering in search of heaven. When one of the judges told him they knew he was a spy sent ahead by the king of Spain to conquer the kingdom of Japan, Brother Giordano replied:

"They have deceived you and lied to you, and the reason is evident and clear, for if I come here first and foremost to make a Christian of your king and then the others, and my king desires the same, and both of us are motivated by the love that both he and I have for you all, as prescribed by Christian law which is wholly based on love, then it is clear that we do not intend to deprive you of your kingdom: that would mean we came for our own personal interest and that we did not wish you well but evil."

Seeing that they were not getting anywhere, the judges decided to have the two friars taken to prison, not far from the tribunal. They were locked up in a sort of square cage eight ells long, with a grid made of great poles through which the guards could always observe them, while they could not communicate with the other imprisoned Christians, who were in such need of a word of encouragement, the Sacraments, a blessing. The friars were forbidden to celebrate Mass, which would have given them great comfort. To eat they had only a little salted radish, almost raw, and, instead of bread, rice, also not properly boiled; sometimes they would get a salted sardine.

Whilst in prison Brother Giordano meditated on what he had done and his miraculous recovery, and wishing a record of it to remain, he described it in another letter, which he wrote as best he could with a brush, as he had no pen:

I managed two forays into the kingdoms close to Nagasaki: the first time I ventured into places where no missionary had set foot for the previous eight years. I confessed many people and comforted others. I returned another time and with the help of a good guide managed to reach all parts of Omura, and this time I converted an infidel and confessed people who had not confessed for twenty years...

Then the good Lord, as part of His great design, had me fall ill of a sickness so dangerous I thought I was going to die of it. I was thus compelled to return to Nagasaki, whence I had fled. But after four or five days I recovered, the Most Holy Virgin having healed me, after I had begged her with all my might to give me strength until they killed me for Christ: that was my only reason for wishing health and life.

Brother Giordano also provided information about his work *De divinis judiciis*, which had been confiscated; he had also written as best he could a *Tract* on the Martyr Saints, in Latin, which he had left in the house of the butler of the Rosary.

XIII.
She Too Had the Right to Die with her Father Giordano

Word of the two Dominicans' arrest immediately spread everywhere, reaching the remotest areas where Christians had gone into hiding. It also reached Madeleine of Nagasaki, a young Dominican Tertiary, originally from a village near that city; after her parents had been torn from her before being condemned to martyrdom for their faith, she had taken a vow of perpetual virginity before an image of the Rosary and had devoted her life wholly to the Lord. And in order not to deny the Lord she had fled to the mountains and with other Christians spent her time praying, performing acts of charity, and reading devotional works, for she could read and write the Latin language.

Brother Giordano had been her spiritual father and confessor and in less than two years had confessed her three times, no mean task in those days of persecution, with all the work that the few remaining Fathers had to do in Nagasaki. He had given her the habit of the Third Order of Saint Dominic and the hope of taking her vows; by now everyone called her Blessed. But now that Brother Giordano was in prison, how could she take her vows?

As soon as she knew of his arrest, she went straight to the prison, confronted the guards, and declared that she too was a Christian and a sister, a disciple of Brother Giordano, and that she should be imprisoned and die with her spiritual father. The guards sent her away, saying she was a weak young woman who could not bear the torture reserved to missionaries; Sister Madeleine insisted they should take her, but they would not listen.

She therefore went to the tribunal in Nagasaki and repeated that they should respect her right to die along with the man who had admitted her to the Order; the judges seemed to wish to grant her request and ordered her arrest, hoping however that she would change her mind.

She was offered riches and a high-ranking husband if only she renounced her faith. Then, to break her, they tortured her in several ways. They hung her by the arms to the gallows and after some time the judges returned to ask her once again if she had changed her mind; but she did not falter, replying instead with a laugh that she was sorry they had treated her like a child, with such mild torture, and that they could be assured that even with the most atrocious of torments she would remain steadfast and never deny Christian law. Then they subjected her to a torture consisting of sharp canes being inserted between her nails and the flesh and bone of her fingers, ordering her to scratch the earth with them. She bore that too. The tyrant could not tolerate being defeated and ridiculed, and by a woman too, especially since he had promised the Emperor that he would make all Christians surrender, which was the condition for his obtaining the governorship of Nagasaki. They strung her up by the feet with her head in a container full of water and subjected her again and again to the torture of swallowing water and being violently forced to vomit it up.

The judges could not understand how such a young and beautiful woman could renounce life and all the promises they had made her; they asked her repeatedly if she would give up her religion. Madeleine remained unwavering and repeated that she would rather die a thousand times than renounce her Christian faith.

She was in the prison during the days when Brother Giordano was there, as she wished, but she never had the consolation of taking her vows, which she so ardently wished for, as they would not allow her to see him.

In early October 1634 she was condemned to the scaffold and the pit, with other Japanese Christians. She was led on horseback through the streets of Nagasaki, a rope round the neck and her hands tied behind her back. Hanging on the scaffold with her head in the pit, wearing the habit of a Tertiary of Saint Dominic, she held out for thirteen days and a half, without eating or drinking: truly amazing! Whenever anyone asked her how she felt, she replied that the Lord gave her strength and that she could feel a hand on her face that gave relief to her whole body. Now and again the guards would check to see if she was still alive and they would be furious because they feared their superiors might suspect that other Christians were giving her succor while their backs were turned; they thus decided to deal her a mortal blow to the head. It rained that night, the pit filled up, and the next day they saw she had drowned. Her body was burned, but her memory and the example she had set lived on; they continued to call her the Blessed Lady of Saint Dominic.

Brother Giordano later learned in prison of her martyrdom.

XIV.
Whom Are You Ordering to Trample on This Sacred Image?

Three times Brother Giordano and Brother Thomas were brought out of the jail and forced to walk through the town all the way to the law court, with their hands tied behind them and a rope round their neck, amid the heathens' cries of derision.

The first time the judges attempted to persuade the missionaries to renounce the Christian faith and worship the pagan idols. As always, they offered them money, comforts, and the Emperor's protection. The Fathers were aggrieved to be treated like children or fools. They were being offered, as it were, a morsel from a rotten apple in exchange for renouncing such a vast and rich treasure, that of serving the true God and Master, their Creator. For Him they would give up their lives not once but a thousand times rather than offend Him with a venial sin. Least of all would they commit the enormous offence of worshiping as Gods beings that were not divine.

On this same occasion the judges were also interrogating some Japanese citizens who had acted as interpreters on board certain Portuguese ships. They wanted to find out whether they were heathens or Christians and whether, in their interpreters' role, they had received letters, money, or other items for the missionaries. To put them to the test, the judges threw to the ground an image of the Virgin Mary and ordered them to trample on it. As indeed they were heathens, they did not need to be told twice. But Brother Giordano, desiring to take the image himself and kiss it but not being able to do so because his hands were tied behind his back, tried to put a stop to this sacrilege by throwing himself to the ground face down over the sacred image, so that they would have to trample on him. Brother Thomas attempted to do the same. The judges tried to force Brother Giordano to his feet, hitting him with cudgels and shoving him this way and that. But Brother Giordano, broken in body but resolute in his faith, continued to pronounce words of defiance:

"Whom are you ordering to trample on this sacred image? These are heathens who do not recognize it and therefore have no respect for it! Order us to do so for we know the veneration that is due to this Lady, and you shall see if we trample on it. But these men are as blind as you are."

The second time the judges did not attempt cajolery, realizing now that they were dealing with no ordinary men and that no gift could graze such rocks of fortitude. Thus they tried with threats and torture. First they threatened to fry the missionaries in oil and to roast them alive. To show they were in earnest, they ordered the grills to be prepared. Word immediately spread that that was to be their punishment. But when the judges realized the friars showed no fear, not even at the sight of the grills, they decided to subject them to the water torture.

The missionaries were forced to drink copious amounts of water. When they could imbibe no more, the torturers inserted great funnels in their mouths down to their throats and poured in buckets of water. When the friars were as swollen as wineskins or barrels, they were thrown to the ground and wooden planks were laid over them. Two of the torturers would then jump on them and press down until water started pouring out of their mouths, ears, noses, eyes, and all the apertures in their bodies.

Then they would immediately start again, pouring water in and forcing it out in the same manner. Sixty buckets Brother Giordano was forced to drink, and Brother Thomas almost as many. The judges wanted to see every single drop come out of their bodies, red with blood, amid indescribable suffering. Finally the missionaries were taken back to jail, more dead than alive, so that they could recover and be fit for further tortures.

The third time the torturers stuck pointed white-hot canes between the nails and the flesh and bone of the missionaries' hands. The sticks were pushed halfway up their fingers. No pain could be worse! But the friars bore the torture and showed no sign of desperation or discouragement. This made the judges think they were not suffering enough and the torturers were therefore ordered to seize the missionaries by the arms and force them to beat the canes against the wall and drive them further into their fingers. But not even that torture made the friars give in. On the contrary, their faces showed an expression of inward joy. The judges were even more enraged and tried to shame them by attacking their modesty. They ordered the torturers to insert a cane in their most private parts, in front of all the spectators. But not even this succeeded and the judges realized that even the most atrocious tortures were just a waste of time. They therefore ordered that the two mangled friars should be taken back to jail, their bodies dripping all over with blood.

Despite everything, some people managed to visit them, talk to them, and even confess in secret. However, it was noticed that the missionaries concealed their hands under their scapular — they did not want to discourage other Christians by displaying the effects of their horrifying torture.

Sister Marina was in jail too. Her crime, like theirs, was that of being a Christian and in addition she had given hospitality to missionaries in her home. She was taken to the tribunal in Omura, where she declared she was a nun. The judges, intrigued by her vow of chastity, resolved to put her to the test in order to see how well she could keep this vow. They had her stripped and made her walk stark naked through the villages in the fief of Omura, where people knew her best. In each town they would tie her to a pole in the public square, with her hands behind her back so that she could not cover herself.

Many were the women who renounced their faith to escape such dishonor and to avoid ending up in a brothel, which was another terrible threat to which these persecutors had recourse. They would rather have been burned alive or suffered any other martyrdom. Even fathers and husbands preferred to yield rather than allow their daughters and wives to be dishonored, while others tried to defend them by force of arms and die with them rather than see them shamed.

For three months and seven days Brother Giordano and Brother Thomas languished in jail, praying and waiting for their sentence to be decided.

XV.
Dux Aliorum Martyrum

On the 11th of November 1634, Martinmas, a day dedicated to devotion to the Most Holy Virgin, sixty-eight people – men and women – were taken out of the prison of Nagasaki to be either burned alive or beheaded, including Brother Giordano and Brother Thomas, who were condemned to death by the scaffold and pit, as well as Sister Marina, who was condemned to die over a slow fire.

They all came out on horseback, their hands tied behind their back and a rope round their neck. The two missionaries led the way, they too with their hands tied in this way and with long poles bearing notices written in Japanese with the death sentence and its motivation, which was that of preaching and teaching the law of Christ in Japan. So that all should know it, the town criers proclaimed it at the top of their voices. They were accompanied by numerous soldiers, torturers, and the judges themselves, who had to witness the deaths or suspend execution if anyone showed signs of wishing to deny his faith.

And so they reached the place of sacrifice, the Holy Mount, less than a quarter of a league from Nagasaki; it could easily be seen from the sea, from the bay where the ships were anchored, several of which belonged to the Portuguese: many of these could see what was happening.

On the Holy Mount the instruments of torture were standing ready in a fenced-off enclosure: poles, knives, pits an arm's length long and two deep, and low gallows over the pits. The pagans flocked to see, and Christians hid among them, kneeling and worshiping the Holy Martyrs. Europeans were forbidden even to watch the executions but many, especially the Portuguese merchants, succeeded in observing them without being seen. They were however risking their lives, although some were brave enough to speak to the missionaries while they were being led to their execution. But how often a moment's danger is worth more than a whole life! And they were able to witness the martyrdom of Brother Giordano and his companions.

As soon as they saw the enclosure, the two friars thanked the Lord for their imminent martyrdom. At once they dismounted, knelt down, and kissed the ground, the pits, and the gallows that had been set up for them: this soil was sacred, washed with the blood of many Martyrs, and now it would be washed with theirs. While the executioners prepared to subject them to the final torture, they bade farewell with powerful voice, crying out the faith for which they were dying, the faith they had preached, and they warned everyone that without faith no one could be saved; they condemned the judges' cruelty and heartened the others who were about to be martyred.

This annoyed the executioners, who interrupted their declarations and threw them to the ground, binding their feet tightly together and hanging them, by the feet, from the gallows, so that their head and half their body were in the pit as far as the waist. Then they quickly wedged a wooden board in by the waist of each one, shutting off the pit, and placed heavy stones over the board to prevent it from shifting. In this state they left the Martyrs, bleeding from the mouth, eyes, nose, and ears.

In the meantime, the flames rose higher and also Sister Marina was burned alive. When the fire was extinguished, her ashes were gathered and scattered in the sea to stop the Christians from worshiping her and the women, who called her "the woman of fortitude", from emulating her.

Hanging in this fashion, bleeding, and without food or water, Brother Giordano remained alive for seven days, *Dux aliorum Martyrum*, to his executioners' great dismay; Brother Thomas, a little less. It was the 17th of November 1634 when the Friar of Santo Stefano passed away; his body too was burned to ashes, so that not even the memory of him should remain.

XVI.
Return

Your name seemed to be lost in the centuries, for ever. Even in your own home village no one knew of you. Then one of your brethren, Father Matteo Angelo Coniglione, historian of the Dominican Province of Sicily, asked the Archpriest Vito Alomia of Ciminna for your baptismal certificate. But silence continued to reign in our village, as if nothing had happened.

Not even the zealous and austere priest Luigi Abella, who for thirty years had been Archpriest of Santo Stefano, had ever heard of you, when others asked for your baptismal certificate and he discovered that you were one of the Dominican Martyrs of Nagasaki and that your brethren were striving to have you proclaimed Blessed and then Saint. But then he did everything in his power. He wrote to Agrigento, to Catania, to Rome, and to France to get information about you: he could not accept the fact that you had so long been completely unknown to your fellow villagers and continued to be so. He read with great excitement the pages written by Father Coniglione, had them duplicated, and gathered them together in a pamphlet, which he distributed at Christmas in 1963; he gave me a copy when I went to visit him for the last time in the institute of nuns that he himself had founded: he was ill and it was not long before he died, without the consolation of seeing you on the altars. He had even commissioned a painter from our village to make a picture of you, to paint what he imagined in his mind, but the painter had unexpectedly died. And when Abbot Estournet, the parish priest of Sérignan, came to Santo Stefano and presented the work of another painter, a Protestant, so that the people of Santo Stefano could worship your image, the good and simple Archpriest, showing great emotion in his eyes and words, declared that the French priest had been a benefactor also for Santo Stefano, considering all he had done to help the people of Santo Stefano to find out about their Saint.

Your name once again became familiar to your fellow villagers. Now they listened all agog and repeated to one another your sufferings, your tortures, and your martyrdom and they were amazed that for so long no one had spoken of you. The long wait had begun.

Prelates, major and minor, came to the town as well as scholars and others driven by mere curiosity, but they could find nothing new about you. Yet the archives of the Mother Church contained numerous documents mentioning you and your family; the parish records show the registration of your baptism, later copied out again, of your parents' wedding and deaths, and of your little brothers' baptisms and their deaths too, as also of your name as a godfather: all this and much more besides I was able to read in these precious records, to my immense surprise and rare joy, records that are available to all, without any particular effort. And now I myself, after almost four centuries: but why me? It seemed to me an act of grace, my Saint, but why should I be the one to receive it? I communicated my emotion to the diligent, jovial Archpriest Antonino Massaro, who in those days was very close to me as we awaited the extraordinary event.

I had also looked for you in the convents and archives of Spain and I continued my search for you in Agrigento, in Palermo, and in Catania and then in Mexico. I shall look for you for ever.

Your name dazzled the world like a flash of lightning when in Manila, on the 18th of February 1981, the Polish Pope John Paul II proclaimed you Blessed. A few years went by and the same Pope canonized you in Rome, on the 18th of October 1987.

And you returned to your fellow villagers, a Saint, a new Patron for them beside the three ancient Patrons, to those people who still live in places familiar to you and who fall asleep in the same land that harbored your mother and father and your little brothers and your childhood friends.

Of you, these documents remain in your native village, just as the witnesses of the first years of your life still exist – the mountains, the stones, the fields. All trace was lost of the writings to which, far away, you entrusted your thoughts in those few moments when you could write something down, in the brief time conceded to your rest – there we would have found your soul.

But we can see and touch the paper on which you laid your holy hand to record the baptisms you performed with such joy in Manila. These are your relics and they say much about you, about your strong personality as a fervid man of God; they tell of your commitment to the life of an exemplary missionary, your greatest work, to which you dedicated your life and for which you died, as you wished. Your martyrdom and your death tell us everything of you.

O beloved Giordano, I do not see you in the portraits that modern painters have made of you. I have found you, felt you, in the ancient, silent convents; in the places I began to know as a child; when I listened again to the songs of our peasants behind the Mother Church of Our Lady of Sorrows of Calvary, where you were baptized, when I admired the moon rising over our mountains and that majestic crest that climbs high, straight, and solemn, rolling gently up to the peak of San Calò.

To Saint Giordano of Santo Stefano

Your mountains my mountains
scented with mint and oregano
as a child I started
to climb them
grasping the steep cliffs
breathing the fragrance of the earth
thinking more of the dead than of the living,
I gazed upon the village down below
for ever torn by hatred
drenched over and over again in the blood
of human wickedness,
and in tears,
where all forgot you
and your name was lost in time.
I wondered at the flocks of sparrows
circling in the sky
and listened to the voice of the wind
the babbling of the water
the sweet rustling of the trees:
they told me of you.
I have found you again
in the places of my distant childhood,
At Rosario, Maddalena,
Quisquina, Muntivernu,
Margimutu, Mount San Calò.
I have asked about you in Girgenti and Palermo,
in Saint Stephen of Salamanca
and in other convents in Spain
and in New Spain.
And I will keep on looking for you,

O Giacinto Giordano,
with my memory of you I have lived a better life.
And if you are always next to me,
how can I fear the future?
And when yet again I am dismayed
by human injustice
and I feel weak and alone,
your example will always give me strength.
A man who is a man
is undaunted by his duties,
walks towards the light,
does not turn back
when faced by darkness:
this you showed me.
And when the shadows
shall dispel the last illusions,
when the joyous sun shall no longer wake me
and I shall stand confounded before God,
whom shall I invoke?
You will be with me
as you were with the sick,
and the sinners of Manila,
the martyrs of Nagasaki,
my Saint Giordano.